BEYOND
BIZARRE

FRIGHTENING FACTS & BLOODCURDLING TRUE TALES

VARLA VENTURA

WEISER BOOKS
San Francisco, CA / Newburyport, MA

First published in 2010 by
Red Wheel/Weiser, LLC
With offices at:
500 Third Street, Suite 230
San Francisco, CA 94107
www.redwheelweiser.com

ISBN: 978-1-57863-464-4

Library of Congress Cataloging-in-Publication Data

Ventura, Varla, 1958-
Beyond bizarre : frightening facts & bloodcurdling true tales / Varla
Ventura.
p. cm.
Includes bibliographical references.
ISBN 978-1-57863-464-4 (alk. paper)
1. Curiosities and wonders. I. Title.
AG243.V42 2010
001.9—dc22
2010014732

Cover and text design by Sara Gillingham
Typeset in Antihistory, Toronto Gothic, and Rough Egyptienne
Cover illustrations: Skeleton, Spider, Turtle and Squid © Dover. Woman and parasol,
moth © Miss Mary. Magician © Pepin Press.
Interior illustrations: p10,12,13,15,16,17,19,21,23,24,25,60,87 © Dover; p72,78,82 ©
istockphoto.com; p13,30,36,42,75,77,83,214,264,285,291 © Dreamstime.com; p38,39,4
3,55,62,69,90,93,98,106,108,111,116,119,122,128,129,132,142,147,162,169,170,177,183,1
99,205,210,221,224,225,229,230,232,234,235,240,242,243,244,249,250,253,256,260,2
70,270,273,274,277,284,286 © Miss Mary; p31,33,35,41,45,50,53,67,70,73,85,94,106,11
4,115,125,131,150,157,166,200,218,219,233,291 © Pepin.

Printed in Canada
TCP
10 9 8 7 6 5 4 3 2 1

DEDICATED TO THE MANY FRIENDS WHO HAVE
KEPT ME COMPANY IN THE DARKEST HOURS OF THE NIGHT.
V.V.

INTRODUCTION

When we first heard from Varla in *The Book of the Bizarre*, we knew almost immediately that there would be a sequel. Had we printed them all, the amount of freaky facts she had provided for the first book would have spilled out of its pages, and we had to make careful selections to keep the book from becoming "too much of a good thing." But we never forgot how many medical maladies and Hollywood twists of fate there were lying on the cutting room floor. It just seemed natural that Varla should write *Beyond Bizarre* with new chapters and even more unusual trivia and terrifying tales. It gives us great pleasure to think of her writing in the wee hours of the morning, her black cat curled up at her feet, the wind rattling the windows of her Victorian attic apartment. There is something of us in Varla, and we can see her terrifying generations to come—if by no other means than having such a keen eye for irony, wickedness, and the outright strange. We hope you enjoy *Beyond Bizarre* as much as we have.

Amber Guetebier and Rachel Leach
Editors at Large
Weiser Books

CONTENTS

1. YO, HO AND UP SHE RISES: STORIES FROM THE SEA

SHIPWRECKS, GHOST SHIPS,
SEA CREATURES, PIRATES, AND OCEAN LORE.

The loud wind never reached the ship,
Yet now the ship moved on!
Beneath the lightning and the Moon
The dead men gave a groan.
—SAMUEL TAYLOR COLERIDGE,
THE RIME OF THE ANCIENT MARINER

THE CREAKING PLANK OF A FOG-SOAKED WHARF, the shadow of a ghost ship slipping silently out of harbor, legends of tentacles that can pull down a merchant vessel—the ocean is as vast in stories and legends as it is in size. From the lobster pot soul cages that rattle with drowned men to the phosphorescent glimmer of the vampire squid's false eyes, chilling tales and creepy creatures are part of the sea's endless mysteries.

I have called a port town home for a number of years, and the sound of the foghorns reminds me that the murky waters still churn, still push their foggy fingers against the windowpanes, and still send out their siren songs and ghoulish stories from hilltop to deep crevasse. And so I welcome you, dear reader, to the monstrous and the mysterious, the dark and the stormy, the oozing and the beautiful, in this totally bizarre chapter.

FANCY A SPOT OF MONSTER SPOTTING?

Members of Victorian England's middle class thought it fashionable to go "monster spotting," or trolling for sea creatures.

THE DEVIL SEA CREATURE OF ORKNEY

The Orkney Islands, off the northern tip of Scotland, are said to be home to one of the nastiest sea creatures in history: the sea-trow. This monkey-faced, flat-footed, scaly beast terrified 18th- and 19th- century sailors and land dwellers alike. It was said to make frequent waddling visits ashore to visit—and haunt—the island townspeople. Courtesy of Orkneyjar (*orkneyjar.com*), the Orkney folklore goes:

> *The Fishers both in Orkney and Zetland are affraid when they see them, which panick fear of their's makes them think and sometimes say that it is the Devil in the shape of such Creatures, whether it be so or not as they apprehend, I cannot determine. However, it seems to be more than probable, that evil spirits frequent both Sea and Land.*

CEPHALOPOD HEAVEN

➢ The octopus is considered the most intelligent of all invertebrates. It has both short- and long-term memory, and has been observed using tools, like coconut shells, for shelter.

➢ When an octopus gets stressed out, it may eat its own legs—though some say this tendency is caused by a virus that is exacerbated by stress.

➢ The largest giant Pacific octopus (*Octopus dofleini*) ever caught weighed in at 600 pounds!

➢ The octopus has no bones. The only hardened part of its body is its beak, which is made of the same type of material as human fingernails.

➢ Octopus blood is light blue.

➢ "*Cephalopod*" means "head to foot"; in other words, the creature's legs are attached to its head.

➢ Octopuses are able to change both their skin color *and* skin texture to camouflage themselves and thus fool predators.

➢ Early seafarers called the octopus the "devil-fish" because of its frightful appearance.

➢ The sting of the blue-ringed octopus (*Hapalochlaena maculosa*) causes paralysis and even death.

Flotsam: Goods that float after being thrown over-board at sea or in case of shipwreck. Jetsam or jettison: Castaway goods that sink.

———— ✦ ————

A giant squid caught in 1878 weighed more than 4,000 lbs and had thirty-five-foot-long tentacles.

———— ✦ ————

The smallest crustacean in the world is the aptly named pea crab, which measures about 2.5 inches. The largest crustacean is the giant spider crab, whose body can grow between 12 and 14 inches across, with a claw span of 7.8 to 8.8 feet!

———— ✦ ————

The oldest living sea anemone was 80 years old, and the oldest clam, 200 years.

———— ✦ ————

The term "fathom" is an old nautical word used to measure the depth of the water. One fathom is six feet, a measurement based on the length from a sailor's fin-gertip to fingertip when his arms were outstretched.

SEMBLANCE OF A SAILOR

The U.S. frigate *Constellation* creaks and groans on its moorings in the Baltimore harbor. But visitors to this historic ship, built in 1797 and used as the first man-of-war in the U.S. naval fleet, have heard and seen more than just seagulls and the sound of gentle waves. The ghost of an old sailor named Neil Harvey, in the garb of yesteryear, appears to visitors. The ghosts of Captain Thomas Truxtun and an unnamed watchman who fell asleep on duty and was executed, reputedly by being strapped to a ship's gun and blown to smithereens, are said to also haunt this ship.

TOUGH AS NAILS

The phrase "I'll nail you for that" comes from a rather gruesome punishment for crimes committed at sea. The accused would be nailed to the ship's mast by his earlobes and left until nightfall.

SWEET, SWEET JANE

Blackbeard the pirate was captured on board his ship, *Jane*, by Lieutenant Robert Maynard. Maynard cut off Blackbeard's head with a cutlass and then threw the corpse overboard. Legend has it that the corpse swam around the ship three times before sinking into the watery depths below. Blackbeard's head was tied to the bow of the *Jane*.

Around a cape he once would sail,
And thus it was that he did hail:
"'I'll sail, I'll sail, I'll sail
evermore!'"
Huzza! Satan, he heard him hail!
ho! heigho!
Huzza! Satan took him by his word!
ho! heigho!
Huzza! And damned he! His ship,
she leaps from wave to wave forever,
evermore!"

—RICHARD WAGNER, *THE FLYING DUTCHMAN*

THE WICKEDEST CITY

During the golden age of piracy, many a port town played host to the debauchery and dubious delights of sailing types. But one city in particular, Port Royal in Jamaica, was known as the "richest and wickedest city in the world." Perhaps called so because of its extensive selection of taverns, brothels, and various illegal or illicit activities, Port Royal is now a premier destination for tourists.

And, sick of prey,
yet howling on for more,
Vomitest they wrecks
on its inhospitable shore!
Treacherous in calm,
and terrible in storm,
Who shall put forth on thee,
Unfathomable sea?
—PERCY BYSSHE SHELLEY, "UNFATHOMABLE SEA"

SEA CREATURES ON PARADE

⋏ Ever wonder how clownfish can tolerate living among stinging sea anemones? Their entire bodies are slathered with a layer of mucus that insulates their bodies against big stings.

⋏ The goblin shark got its name from the shape of its nose. The shark's long, trowel-shaped snout protrudes from the head like a sword, giving the shark a kind of mutated hammerhead look.

⋏ The scorpion fish has a tricky way of catching its prey. Its dorsal fin, on the top of its back, is shaped like a smaller fish, which lures medium-size fish right into its jaws.

⋏ The mighty oarfish, which can grow to lengths of 56 feet, is one of the longest fish in the ocean. Its snake-like appearance and prominent dorsal fin might account for early sailors' sea serpent myths.

⋏ The orange sea pen got its name because it resembles—uncannily so—an old-fashioned quill pen. These soft corals can grow to be 5 feet tall.

DEADBEAT FISH

The male deep-sea anglerfish definitely doesn't wear the pants in his relationship. Significantly smaller than his female counterpart, the male permanently attaches himself to his mate's abdomen, living as a parasite for the rest of his life.

DEEP-SEA DRACULA

The *Vampyroteuthis infernalis*, a name that literally translates as the "vampire squid from hell," is a big name for a benign little creature. The 15-centimeter (6-inch) squid lives in an oxygen-minimum zone 600 to 900 meters (656 to 984 yards) deep, a depth that fosters the spookiest of sea creatures. But this squid is equipped with neat biological adaptations to help it thrive down there: its blue blood is oxygen rich, pulsing through the small body faster than the normal red kind, and the squid's muscles are weak, which preserves energy. But by far the vampire squid's coolest ability is to disorient potential predators with flashes of light; its body is almost completely covered with light-producing organs called photophores.

THE MIGHTY KRAKEN

Norse seamen of the 13th to 19th centuries called their sea monsters kraken. Over time, the creatures were variously described as gargantuan, tentacled, and squid- or crablike, but by the eighteenth century, they were mostly known as malevolent, octopuslike monsters. Kraken were capable of felling large ships, especially with the whirlpool effect their island-sized bodies created when they quickly descended back into the ocean.

Kraken were also known to create excellent fishing conditions for fishermen; it was said that they spent three months eating and three months digesting their meals, and for this period of time, they stayed dormant at the bottom of the ocean. For snacks, the kraken fed on a fish entourage that stayed with them to feed off their monstrous excrement.

But when kraken elected to travel to the sea surface, all hell broke loose, as Swede Jacob Wallenberg wrote in 1781: "Gradually, Kraken ascends to the surface, and when he is at ten to twelve fathoms, the boats had better move out of his vicinity, as he will shortly thereafter burst up, like a floating island, spurting water from his dreadful nostrils and making ring waves around him, which can reach many miles. Could one doubt that this is the Leviathan of Job?"

The legend of kraken has been immortalized in literature, film, and song over hundreds of years. Tennyson wrote a poem called "The Kraken," and it is said that Jules Verne drew heavily on kraken imagery in imagining the squid lair in his *Twenty Thousand Leagues Under the Sea*. The kraken makes an appearance in C. S. Lewis's *Narnia* series, and there is a kraken supervillain in Marvel comics. The kraken is portrayed as a horrendous sea creature in the 21st century *Pirates of the Caribbean* movie series, and is a noted character in the *Final Fantasy* video games series. Finally, at SeaWorld Orlando, there is a rollercoaster called the Kraken—a truly terrifying ride!

THE ARCTIC APPARITION

On October 1, 1931, the cargo steamer *Baychimo*, returning from its trade journey to the Canadian coastline, became immovably stuck in a block of pack ice off the coast of Alaska. Its crew abandoned the ship and traveled several miles over the ice to seek shelter in nearby Barrow, but they returned several days later when the ship was shaken free from the ice. Alas, just seven days later, it became mired again, and most of its crew were rescued via aircraft. Others stayed behind, resolved to wait out the winter, so devoted were they to the *Baychimo*. But all traces of the barge were lost following a treacherous November blizzard. The crewmen assumed it had sunk, but after an Inuit trader told them he'd seen it floating some 45 miles from where they camped, they found the ship, unloaded their valuables, and left.

Over the next 30 years, there were many sightings, and even a couple boardings, of the crewless and empty *Baychimo*. It was seen floating in a 100-mile radius of where it had first been trapped, and remained intact despite stormy and frigid weather. In 2006, the Alaskan government opened an investigation into the fate of the ship, which is now presumed to have sunk.

The largest U.S. naval ship ever to disappear without a trace was the USS *Cyclops*, a 19,360-ton collier. In March 1918, on a return voyage from Brazil, the ship and all its hands vanished, and the wreckage was never recovered.

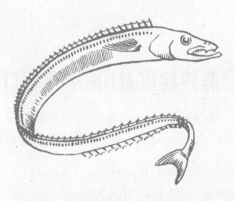

HARMFUL UNDER THE SEA

Of the more than 3,700 World War II shipwrecks still at the bottom of the Pacific Ocean, many contain the remnants of toxic cargo, such as oil, diesel, gasoline, and chemicals. These harmful pollutants have the potential to wipe out ecosystems and spoil beaches, and, in doing so, influence the economies of the affected countries.

THE PRACTICALITIES OF PIRACY

➤ Pirates didn't wear gold hoop earrings for fashion—they did so to ensure they could afford a proper burial.

➤ Pirates sustained themselves through months on the high seas by imbibing alcohol—lots of it. Alcohol was safer to drink than the "fresh" water the ships carried, which often carried illnesses and grew slimy from months in wooden barrels. A favorite alcohol was rum, which was also called "grog," "the pirates' drink," "kill-devil," "demon water," and "Barbados water."

➤ Most of the treasure captured by pirates didn't last long enough to get buried. It was spent on gambling, women, and alcohol.

U.S. NAVY: IN LEAGUE WITH SEA MONSTERS?

In the summer of 1997, underwater microphones placed in the ocean by the U.S. Navy detected an ultra low-frequency sound whose source has remained a mystery. The sound, which became known as the Bloop, was detected several times over a range of 5,000 kilometers. Scientists say the Bloop matches the sound profile of a living creature, but they have yet to identify which one. The Bloop is too big and powerful to have been made by a whale. In fact, scientists don't know of any animal on earth that could have made the sound—unless it's an animal that hasn't been discovered yet. Maybe a kraken?

DOIN' IT FOR THE FAMILY

Pirates used nicknames so that government officials couldn't persecute their relatives on land.

ROCK OPERA

Many people have heard the story of the *Flying Dutchman,* the ship captained by a man who was condemned to sail the seas for eternity. But few know of his curser, the aquatic demon queen Rockalda. She is portrayed as the evil spirit of the deep in a 19th century opera about the *Dutchman*. In the opera, the wicked Rockalda only lets the wretched captain ashore on the condition that he promises to periodically sacrifice a maiden at sea.

THE LIONESS OF BRITTANY

The year was 1343, and Lady Jeanne de Belleville was living peacefully with her husband and two sons in the countryside of Brittany. As they often were, the Bretons were at war with the French and the British—who were also at war with each other—and there was tension in the air. Lady Jeanne's husband was accused of siding with the British, and he was he hastily imprisoned and executed by the French. Distraught, Lady Jeanne sought revenge for her husband's death. She sold all of her assets, which were many, and used the cash to purchase a fleet of three ships with which to terrorize the French navy. Her ships cruised the coast of Normandy, seizing French ships and killing their crews. Dubbed the Lioness of Brittany for the merciless terror she wrought on all things French, Lady de Belleville was one of the best-known female pirates to sail the open seas.

PIRATE SOUL MUSEUM

According to its website, the Pirate Soul Museum, located in Florida, is "the largest and most authentic collection of pirate artifacts under one roof." It boasts the 1699 journal from Captain Kidd's last voyage, an authentic treasure chest, and real pirate flags, among other pirate gems.

BURIAL AT SEA

A company in Sarasota, Florida, offers a unique underwater service: the opportunity to be buried at sea. Eternal Reefs will take your ashes and incorporate them into a coral reef off the coast of Florida.

A Captain bold in Halifax,
Who dwelt in country quarters,
Seduced a maid who hanged herself
One morning in her garters,
His wicked conscience smited him,
He lost his stomach daily,
He took to drinking turpentine
And thought upon Miss Bailey.
Oh, Miss Bailey, unfortunate Miss Bailey,
Oh, Miss Bailey, unfortunate Miss Bailey,
One night, betimes he went to bed,
For he had caught a fever,
Said he, "I am a handsome man
And I'm a gay deceiver."
His candle just at twelve o'clock
Began to burn quite palely,
A ghost stepped up to his bedside
And said, "Behold! Miss Bailey."
Oh, Miss Bailey, unfortunate Miss Bailey,
Oh, Miss Bailey, unfortunate Miss Bailey,
"Avaunt, Miss Bailey," then he cried,

"You can't fright me really."
"Dear Captain Smith," the ghost replied,
"You've used me ungenteelly.
The Coroner's quest was hard with me
Because I've acted frailly,
And parson Biggs won't bury me
Though I'm a dead Miss Bailey."
Oh, Miss Bailey, unfortunate Miss Bailey,
Oh, Miss Bailey, unfortunate Miss Bailey,
"Dear Ma'am," said he, "since you and I
Accounts must once for all close,
I have a one pound note in my
Regimental small clothes.
'Twill bribe the Sexton for your grave."
The ghost then vanished gaily,
Crying, "Bless you wicked Captain Smith,
Remember poor Miss Bailey."
Oh, Miss Bailey, unfortunate Miss Bailey,
Oh, Miss Bailey, unfortunate Miss Bailey,
—TRADITIONAL SIXTEENTH-CENTURY SEA SONG,
GEORGE COLMAN

2. IT'S ENOUGH TO MAKE YOU HURL

CRAZY CARNIVALS, FANTASTIC FREAK SHOWS, HAUNTED AMUSEMENT PARKS, SCARY RIDES, AND CREEPY CLOWNS

> I remain just one thing, and one thing only,
> and that is a clown.
> —CHARLIE CHAPLIN

I LOOKED FORWARD EVERY AUGUST TO THE county fair that would be erected in a field on the outskirts of town. It was a sticky and laughter-filled event—cotton-candy mouths and squeals of terror, flashing lights, and mechanical doors swinging open to reveal a haunted house's shadowy interior. I remember the first time I was allowed to roam free of my parents. I stumbled around, drunk on the pink-popcorn-scented air, too thrilled to even get on a ride. I couldn't stay away, and I rode my bike back out to the field just a week later, hoping to hop the fence and take advantage of the Tilt-a-Whirl for the first time. Though I knew the fair was a fleeting event, I hadn't realized it would be gone so soon, and by the time I arrived, the carnival had packed up, leaving behind the remnants of balloons and candy wrappers, the tracks of trailer hitches, and collapsed bumper cars.

My love of the gypsy-clown life of carnivals never died. Circus freaks, sideshows, amusement parks, fairs, and later even the whirl of the casino all find their place in this chapter.

MERRY-GO-ROUND

The word *carousel* is derived from an equestrian sport played in 12th century Arabia and Turkey. The game involved clay balls full of perfumed water being tossed from one horseman to another, who attempted to catch the balls without dropping or breaking them, all while riding. Three hundred years later, this game was performed in France and Germany by cavalrymen as entertainment, and it was expanded into part of a tournament held in a ring. Today's carousels were once referred to as galloping-horse roundabouts.

ONE BOARD SHORT

In Missouri in 1980, a 26-year-old man was killed when he hid in the car of a roller coaster, hoping to ride a second time for free. The operator, believing the cars to be empty, switched the rails so that the train went into a service area. The low clearance of this area caused the young man's head to be crushed between the back of the car's seat and a low beam.

HIGH AS A KITE

The great French tightrope walker Charles Blondin (1824–1897) once sat down to dine at a table and chair balanced on a three-inch rope that was stretched across Niagara Falls. He was also able to walk backwards on the rope, walk on the rope while on stilts, and walk on it while carrying a man on his back. Blondin lived to the ripe age of 72, when he died peacefully in his bed.

Hans Langseth's beard is on view at the Smithsonian in Washington, D.C. Why? It is the longest beard recorded—17.5 feet (5.3 m) long, although some sources claim the beard was over 18 feet (about 5.5 m) long. Langseth lived from 1846 to 1927, and his beard was cut off when he died. The Smithsonian Institution has had the beard since 1967, although it is not always on display.

THE SHOW MUST GO ON . . .

Circus founder P. T. Barnum died around 6:30 p.m. on April 7, 1891. Although word of his imminent death had come to his partner, James A. Bailey days before, the show did, in fact, go on that evening. The day of the funeral, however, refunds or exchanges were offered, as the circus did not perform.

ON THE ROCKS

In 1564, 1608, 1684, 1739, 1788, and 1814, England's Thames River was host to the Thames Frost Fair. Held atop the then-wider and frozen-solid river, this winter-time extravaganza was one of history's most distinctive. The fair featured all manner of activities, including puppetry, sledding, and ice-skating. Booths of all kinds, selling wares and foods, and even a printing press were erected on the ice.

A man was killed on Coney Island's "Cyclone" roller coaster in 1985, when he got the bright idea to stand up during a ride and was knocked in the head by a crossbeam.

THE COMISKEY CURSE

Named for the original owner of the Chicago White Sox, Charles Comiskey, the Comiskey Curse is said to have begun in 1910 with the opening of Comiskey Park. Even before the park's gates opened to the general public, there were problems. Construction was delayed for five weeks because of a steelworker's strike. And the day before the park was to open, a worker fell from the roof and died. The White Sox lost their first game in the new home stadium, and three players were injured in the first three days of the park's official opening.

Comiskey's reputation was that of a man who was anything but generous, and many blame his stinginess as the motivation for the Black Sox Scandal: a fixed game that guaranteed a loss at the 1919 World Series. The Comiskey Curse seemed to grow after this ill-fated game, causing years of devastating losses of games and key players. Among the specific players affected by the curse was Johnny Mostil, who, in 1927, had an affair with his teammate Red Faber's wife and then attempted suicide during spring training. He used a razor to slash his wrists and chest. All-star pitcher Monte Stratton lost his leg during a hunting accident in 1938, and in 1940, second baseman Jackie Hayes lost his sight from an infection in his eye.

When Charles Comiskey died in 1931, his son, Louis, took over the team. But Louis's life was cursed when, at age 27, he contracted scarlet fever. He lived to be 54, but not without being encumbered by numerous health problems brought about by the earlier illness.

The Comiskey Curse was blamed for White Sox's continuing significant losses and bad luck through the 1950s. Bill Veeck, who came to own the team in 1959 and who suffered his own string of ill luck, decided to stage Anti-Superstition Night at Comiskey Park on May 14, 1977. The event featured witches atop the dugout, putting hexes on the Cleveland Indians (whom the Sox would play the next day); mirrors to break and ladders to walk under; and even an organ-grinder monkey. And it seemed to work, because the next night, the White Sox beat the Indians 18–2.

The White Sox did fare better in the early 1980s and the early 1990s, but it wasn't until the 2005 World Series victory that the curse seemed to finally have been lifted.

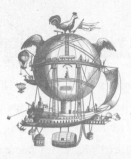

SOME OF THE SCARIEST AMUSEMENT PARK RIDES TODAY

- The X-Scream, perched at the top of the Stratosphere Hotel in Las Vegas, holds riders facedown over the edge of the tallest observation tower in the United States. Riders stare 866 feet down at the little drunken ants cavorting around Vegas.

- The Kingda Ka, at Six Flags in New Jersey, and Top Thrill Dragster, at Cedar Point Amusement Park in Ohio, are the fastest roller coasters in the world. They take riders up 40 feet and "drop" them; during the drop, riders reach speeds of 120 mph.

- For anyone with a fear of heights, the Skycoaster is a true nightmare. Riders are clamped to a wire hanging between two towers. Then they are forced to pull their own ripcord, falling more than 100 feet before the wire stops them.

TAKE THAT, PARIS!

George Washington Gale Ferris (1859–1896), a bridge builder from Pittsburgh, Pennsylvania, was commissioned in 1892 to build something to rival the Eiffel Tower for the World's Fair in Chicago. At 264 feet high, supported by 140-foot towers, and connected by a 45-foot axle, the world's first Ferris wheel was invented! The same Ferris wheel was dismantled and reassembled for the 1904 St. Louis Exposition. Though it was decommissioned two years later, its legend was known throughout the land.

We are in the same tent as the clowns and the freaks—that's show business. —EDWARD R. MURROW

BIG DADDY

In May 2004, a man too obese to secure the safety harness across the car of a roller coaster in a Boston amusement park was killed when he fell 300 feet to the ground.

HOLD ON TO YOUR HAT!

When the safety announcement at Six Flags tells you to secure your personal belongings before the ride starts, you'd better take it seriously. A 17-year-old boy visiting Six Flags Over Georgia in June 2008 with his church group was decapitated by the Batman Ride after he hopped a couple security fences to recover his hat, which had fallen off during the ride. This was the second Batman Ride–related death at Six Flags Over Georgia.

BANJO THE CLOWN CHANGES HIS MIND ABOUT KILLING FAMILY

A wealthy British socialite was jailed after hiring a circus clown named Banjo to kill her stepson and her husband's ex-wife. Unfortunately for her, Banjo the Clown changed his mind about the hit and went to the police. The defendant, who drove a Mercedes and flew her own plane, claimed she had paid Banjo £1,150 in cash for "surveillance" of her husband.

EXTRA, EXTRA! READ ALL ABOUT IT!

Though many circus workers consider themselves bona fide "freaks," certain national newspapers make millions publicizing the existence of particularly bizarre mutants. Here are some plucked straight from the headlines:

- Half-man; Half-alligator!

- Redneck Vampire Attacks Trailer Park!

- The Amazing Clay Man!

- Aliens Create Man-Martian!

- Man Hatches from Egg!

- Mermaid Cemetery Discovered!

- Time-Travel Dog from Future Held Captive!

- Find Us a Husband, Beg Sexy Siamese Twins!

- Half-Human, Half-Bat Locked Up in Medical Lab!

JOINED BY THE STERNUM, CONNECTED AT THE HEART

These days most Siamese twins have the option of attempting surgical separation at birth, but back in the early 1800s, there wasn't a choice for two guys born joined at the hip. Chang and Eng Bunker were the original sideshow Siamese twins, and they were actually joined at the sternum by a piece of cartilage. Their livers were fused together, but each organ worked independently.

The Changs developed a killer business model, traveling the world to put themselves on exhibition. They finally settled down in North Carolina, of all places, and adopted the surname "Bunker." They bought slaves, set up a farm, and even got married—to two sisters born and raised in North Carolina. For a time the twins and their wives all shared a bed made for four, but the sisters were prone to bickering, and soon two separate households were set up. The brothers would alternate three nights a week at each home, during which time they were apparently very busy: Chang's wife had ten children, and Eng's wife had eleven.

The story of Chang and Eng's death is rather touching: Chang contracted pneumonia and died suddenly in his sleep. Rather than undergo an emergency separation from his dead brother, Eng stuck by Chang's side and passed away three hours after his brother. The twins' liver is preserved in a museum in Pennsylvania.

An amusing procrastination activity is looking at photographs of old-time circus freaks from the early 19th century. Although there's no Photoshop wizardry involved, the photos are quite obviously fake. The rendering of the four-legged girl is clearly just a tall girl sitting in a chair with a small child sitting in her lap, hidden beneath her petticoats. The Wolfman might be slightly more hirsute than the average guy, but a lot of the old-fashioned version of airbrushing went into creating his press photo. And Camel Girl is just very, very flexible. Of course, not all the photos are doctored. Many circus freaks, like the Elephant Man and the Crab Boy, were just people with physical deformities or odd medical conditions.

NOTHING, NOT EVEN NET

The first flying trapeze artist was Jules Léotard, who, in 1856, attached cables and a metal bar to the air vents above the pool in his parents' gym and swung from them. He wore a skin-tight, torso-shaped suit, which came to be known as the leotard.

A kind of holy grail for the tightrope-walking community is the crossing of Niagara Falls. Walkers scale the 1,100-foot gorge directly below the falls, holding only a long stick for balance. Stephen Peer had performed the feat several times, but the falls walk got the best of him in 1887. He and some friends had been drinking, and when he attempted a repeat performance, he fell to his death.

DUMBO'S REVENGE

An African elephant who'd lived most of her life in the circus, Tyke was ready to retire. One day in 1994, she'd simply had enough. In the middle of a live performance, in front of hundreds of spectators, she trampled her trainer, gored her groomer, and escaped, running wild in the streets until she was shot and killed (it took 86 bullets).

Topsy was another circus elephant with a violent streak. She killed three people in three years, including her trainer (who was said to be abusive), and was deemed too dangerous to continue performing. Her owners decided to put her down, but they didn't know how to do it. Their initial plan was to kill her by hanging, but animal-rights groups protested. Finally, Thomas Edison proposed electrocuting the elephant, using alternating current, the same way governments had been executing prisoners for many years. Edison captured the elephant's death, which took a few seconds, on film and later released the film with the title "Electrocuting an Elephant."

THE WORLD'S SADDEST AMUSEMENT PARK

Located in West Virginia, the world's only known haunted amusement park is housed on privately owned land and is accessible only by appointment. The story of the land, which dates back to the late 1700s, is probably as entertaining as the park itself. According to local legend, the first white settler in Mercer Coun-

try was named Mitchell Clay. One day while Clay was out hunting, a band of Native Americans rode up to his land. They killed and scalped one of Clay's boys, killed his sister when she came to her brother's rescue, and kidnapped one other boy, who they later burned at the stake. Clay never forgot the horrible tragedy, and the slain children were buried at the site of their deaths. Hundreds of years later, in the 1970s, the same land was used for a small amusement park and festival space. The park wasn't a moneymaker, and it was abandoned—the Ferris wheel, swings, and buildings left to slowly rot away. It is said that visitors to the spot can hear the voices of children, mixed with carnival laughter, rise up softly in the breeze.

A man billed as Prince Randian was discovered in British Guiana and recruited to work for the circus by P. T. Barnum in 1889. Having no hands or feet, he dressed in a cloth sack and wriggled about on a platform like a snake, earning the nickname Caterpillar Man. His performance included a demonstration of how he shaved his face and how he could roll and light a cigarette using only his mouth. He performed in Barnum's circus for 45 years.

An Indian man known as Laloo was born with a parasitic headless body protruding from his lower breastbone. This baby-sized figure was the result of an incomplete division of the fertilized egg from which he was born; the parasite was his undeveloped, unborn identical twin. While Laloo performed in circus sideshows at the turn of the 20th century, the parasite was dressed as a girl to imply it was his sister. But being his would-be Siamese twin, it was sure to be a male. While the stunted body lacked testicles, it had an undeveloped penis, which Laloo privately boasted had the ability to become erect as well as urinate.

MANE EVENT

Together, the seven daughters of preacher Fletcher Sutherland formed a family band, each playing instruments and singing. However, their real attraction was their mass quantity of hair, which measured to a total of 37 feet (11.3 m). They eventually made a fortune by selling the Seven Sutherland Sisters Hair Grower, a mixture of alcohol, water, and vegetable oil falsely advertised as a rapid hair-growing tonic. The business made $90,000 the first year alone, with the help of

Henry Bailey, a then-employee of the circus who married one of the sisters. The business eventually waned in 1907, when hair fashions turned from long tresses to short bobs.

KILLER CLOWN

John Wayne Gacy was convicted of the rape, murder, and torture of no less than 33 male victims between 1972 and 1978, when he was arrested. He has been dubbed the "Killer Clown" because he worked as an entertainer at children's parties as "Pogo the Clown."

Gacy committed most of his crimes by cruising for young men and luring them to his home, only to torture and kill them. He would also post job advertisements for positions at his construction company and rape and kill the men who came to his house to interview.

Once suspicious police were able to obtain a search warrant to enter Gacy's house, they discovered twenty-nine bodies hidden in a small crawlspace. The victims were all male, ranging in age from 9 to 25. Later, Gacy admitted to more murders and to dumping those bodies in a nearby river. On May 10, 1994, he was executed by lethal injection.

3. HAUNTED HOLLYWOOD

GHOSTLY SETS AND SIGHTINGS,
CELEBRITY DEATHS AND SUPERSTITIONS,
STRANGE COINCIDENCES,
AND HARROWING HORROR FILM FACTS

I love Los Angeles. I love Hollywood. They're beautiful.
Everybody's plastic, but I love plastic. I want to be plastic.
—ANDY WARHOL

OH, HOW THE GHOSTS OF THE GLAMOROUS past still haunt those hills today! Murder, suicide, revenge, traveling ghosts . . . Hollywood lore has been a source of horror for decades. It's not just the specters that appear in hotel mirrors or the whispers heard in movie theaters that make Hollywood so fascinating— it's the *living*, and their impossibly strange habits, odd superstitions, ridiculous demands . . . well, you get the idea. This chapter began with my obsession with old horror movies and deep love for the greats: Bela Lugosi, Lon Cheney, and Boris Karloff. I've included a few good ghost stories to keep your heart pumping, too!

DANG TEENAGERS!

Some people end up *literally* pushing up daisies. Lewis Stone, the 1930s movie star, had a heart attack and fell down dead when he ran out of his house to chase a group of rowdy teenagers out of his garden. He was 73.

Humphrey Bogart is buried with a whistle. He'd given it to Lauren Bacall during the filming of *To Have and Have Not,* their first movie together. She dropped it into his casket right before he was buried. It's inscribed, "If you want anything, just whistle."

IF LOOKS COULD KILL

Lou Tellegen was a dapper young star who appeared in 26 silent films in the 1920s. His good looks brought him fame from Paris to New York, and he was rumored to be Sarah Bernhardt's lover. But when he got cancer in the 1930s, his handsome features rapidly deteriorated. One day, as he stood in the mirror shaving, he was so overcome with horror at his newly ugly face that he stabbed himself to death with a pair of gold scissors that had his name engraved on them.

TOO SCARY

When *The Exorcist* was released in 1974, a man watching it in a theater was so scared that he fainted and broke his jaw on the seat in front of him. He later sued Warner Brothers, the film's production company, for planting subliminal imagery in the film that triggered his fainting. The case was eventually settled out of court for an undisclosed amount of money.

OFF TO SEE THE WIZARD

Clara Bandwick, who played Auntie Em in *The Wizard of Oz* (1939), decided she was off to see the wizard when she started going blind. She had her hair done for the occasion, dressed up in a dressing gown and gold blanket, and lay on a couch with a plastic bag over her head. Her suicide note read: "I am now about to make the great adventure. I cannot endure this agonizing pain any longer. It is all over my body. Neither can I face the impending blindness. I pray the Lord my soul to take. Amen." It's unknown whether she was wearing ruby slippers at the time.

SHOCKING SCENE ALARMS MILLIONS

Psycho (1960) was the first American movie *ever* to show a toilet flushing.

SOMETHING FISHY

In the movie *The Omen* (1976), in the scene where a goldfish bowl falls to the floor and smashes, the goldfish is not real: the director, Richard Donner, refused to kill goldfish for the movie. Instead, dead sardines painted orange were used. PETA would be proud.

THEY SHOULD HAVE KNOWN IT WAS AN OMEN

The sheer number of ominous events that happened to the cast and crew of *The Omen* (1976) is alarming. Gregory Peck's plane was struck by lightning, the director's hotel was bombed, and the dog trainers were attacked by the rottweilers they were training. But here's the kicker: the girlfriend of the special-effects coordinator who masterminded the decapitation scene was actually *decapitated* a few years later while working on the film *A Bridge Too Far* (1977).

→ LITTLE RASCALS OF THE DAMNED ←

Remember that darling black-and-white TV show *The Little Rascals?* Those kids were cute, right? Maybe they even made you wish *you* were a child actor.

Well, be glad you weren't. Those were probably the most accursed rascals in the history of rascalry. Several of the show's child stars met tragic ends.

ALFALFA

After leaving the show, Carl "Alfalfa" Switzer discovered that freckles weren't a qualification for most lines of work. He took jobs as a bartender and hunting guide to make ends meet. One night he got in a drunken scuffle with a friend over a hunting dog, and his "friend" fatally shot Switzer in the stomach.

SLIM

Carl's brother, Harold Switzer, also got shot, but he was the one pulling the trigger. After leaving *The Little Rascals,* he never got another acting role, and he shot himself at the age of 42.

CHUBBY

Norman "Chubby" Chaney weighed in at 300 pounds in his early teens and had surgery to correct a glandular ailment. He died from complications from the surgery at age 18.

WHEEZER

After the show, Robert "Wheezer" Hutchins tried to clean up his act by joining the military. Hilarious hijinks ensued when his B-26 Marauder crashed during a training exercise. He died on impact, at the age of 20.

FROGGY

The shortest-lived of the Little Rascals, the curse caught up with William "Froggy" Laughlin at age 16, when his motor scooter was hit by a truck.

THE POWER OF A PRANK

Some stars are rushed to the hospital for broken limbs or nervous breakdowns. Rumor has it that Richard Gere made a trip to the emergency room at Cedars-Sinai to remove a gerbil that had been shaved, declawed, and inserted up his rectum through a cardboard tube. True story? Probably not. But it's clung to Richard Gere since the 1980s, when an anonymous prankster sent out thousands of "press releases" about the alleged gerbilectomy to fax machines all over Hollywood shortly after the release of *Pretty Woman* (1990).

Bela Lugosi, the actor who famously portrayed Dracula in the 1931 film, was buried wearing his Dracula cape.

CREEPY THEATRICAL SUPERSTITIONS

Many people know that in the theater you should say, "Break a leg" to an actor instead of "Good luck." But you should also watch out for the following theater faux pas, which could result in death, maiming, and bad reviews.

- It's considered bad luck to wear a t-shirt advertising the play before the play opens.

- Many theaters are closed one night a week (usually Monday), allegedly to allow the ghosts that haunt them to put on their own plays.

- It's extremely bad luck to use real money or real jewelry on stage. Most productions use the fake versions.

- Never, ever say "Macbeth" inside a theater. It's said to bring disaster. Theater people call it "The Scottish Play" instead.

DON'T MESS WITH MADAM

High-end Hollywood madam Heidi Fleiss, convicted of conspiracy, tax evasion, and money laundering in the mid-1990s, always had a competitive instinct. As a child, she was a city-wide chess champion, and she dropped out of high school at 16 to bet at the racetrack full time. She got started in the escort business when she worked for Los Angeles's Madam Alex to pay off a $450 gambling debt. When Madam Alex developed heart disease and diabetes (not to mention charges of pandering), Fleiss staged a coup, taking over the successful business. Checkmate!

MOM KNOWS BEST

The mother of *Rebel Without a Cause* star Natalie Wood was a superstitious Russian woman who had been told by a fortune teller to fear "dark waters." As a child, Natalie was terrified of water, and her fear was intensified by several mysterious water-related accidents on movie sets. While shooting *The Green Promise*, young Natalie had to walk over a bridge during a thunderstorm. When she did, the technician flipped a switch prematurely, and the bridge collapsed, throwing Natalie into the treacherous waters and breaking her wrist. When Natalie married Robert Wagner, their honeymoon cruise was cancelled when a violent storm arose. Natalie drowned late one night in 1981 while on a yacht trip off the coast of Catalina Island. The "dark waters" had claimed her at last.

CELEBRITY SUPERSTITIONS

➤ Shania Twain brings her own personal bomb-sniffing dog to her venues.

➤ Christina Aguilera demands a police escort so she doesn't have to get stuck in traffic.

- Tiger Woods believes in the power of red. When he won the Masters in 1997, he was wearing the fiery color.

- Rocker Meat Loaf travels with two stuffed bears.

Many people have heard the story of rock band Van Halen's bizarre demand to have a bowl of M&Ms with all the brown candies taken out placed in every dressing room at every venue where they perform. But according to former lead singer David Lee Roth, nobody in the band has a brown candy phobia. The M&M stipulation is a threshold test designed to verify that the producers are paying very close attention to the fine print in the band's contract. If there are brown M&Ms in the bowl, there might also be a faulty stage set-up, drunken workers, or other contract violations that matter more than wrong-colored chocolate candies.

I used to think as I looked out on the Hollywood night— there must be thousands of girls sitting alone like me, dreaming of becoming a movie star. But I'm not going to worry about them. I'm dreaming the hardest.
—MARILYN MONROE

AT LEAST YOU'LL GROW UP TO BE RICH . . .

Some of the strangest baby names belong to those of the rich and famous.

- Apple: Gwyneth Paltrow and Chris Martin's first daughter

- Audio Science: child of actress Shannyn Sossamon

- Blanket (or Prince Michael II): child of the late Michael Jackson

- Blue Angel: child of U2 lead guitarist The Edge

- Destry: daughter of Steven Spielberg

- Dweezil, Ahmet, Diva Thin Muffin, and Moon Unit: children of the legendary Frank Zappa

- Fifi Trixibelle: daughter of Bob Geldof and the late Paula Yates. Their other daughters are named Peaches Honeyblossom and Pixie

- Heavenly Hiraani Tiger Lily: daughter of Michael Hutchence, lead singer for the band INXS, and Paula Yates

- Jermajesty: child of Jermaine Jackson

- Kyd: child of David Duchovny and Tea Leoni

- Maddox: son of Angelina Jolie and Brad Pitt. Brangelina's other two sons are named Pax and Lennox

- Memphis Eve: daughter of U2 lead singer Bono

- Moxie Crimefighter: child of Penn Jillette, one half of the comedy-and-magic duo Penn and Teller

- Ocean: Forest Whitaker's daughter

- Pilot Inspektor: comedian Jason Lee's child

- Rocket: child of Robert Rodriguez. Siblings: Racer, Rogue, Rebel, and Rhiannon

- Sage Moonblood: Sylvester Stallone's daughter

- Sunday Rose: Daughter of Nicole Kidman and Keith Urban

- Tu Morrow: child of actor Rob Morrow

AS ABOVE, SO BELOW

The Hollywood Forever Cemetery in Hollywood, California, is the final resting place for many famous celebrities, including Rudolph Valentino, Jayne Mansfield, and Douglas Fairbanks Jr. and Sr. But it's more than just a glamorous graveyard. On warm summer nights, the public is invited to picnic with the celebrities as classic movies are screened. DJs spin music before and after the movies, making this garden of the dead anything but lifeless.

Actress Tallulah Bankhead carried a lucky rabbit's foot given to her by her father, and when she died, she was buried with it.

THE CURSE OF THE FAMOUS FILM

According to Michael Largo's *Final Exits*, several films have deadly associations. During the filming of *The Exorcist* (1973), nine people connected with the film died. And four actors from *Poltergeist* movies experienced odd deaths:

- Dominque Dunne, who played the oldest daughter, Dana, in the first film, was choked to death by her ex-lover.

- Heather O'Rourke, who played the youngest daughter, Carol Anne, in the first film, died of a mysterious blood infection.

- Julian Beck, who played a good sprit in the second film, died of stomach cancer shortly after filming.

- Will Sampson, who played the bad spirit in the third film, died during a routine surgery.

At the height of her popularity, actress Mary Pickford (nicknamed "America's sweetheart") earned $10,000 per week. Near the end of the 1920s, she began taking roles that cast her as someone other than the innocent girl she had become famous for. It signaled the end of her career.

Tiny Tim died while singing his signature song "Tiptoe through the Tulips."

Any actress who appears in public without being well groomed is digging her own grave. —JOAN CRAWFORD

STARLET'S SHADOW

If you check in to the Hollywood Roosevelt Hotel, you just might catch a glimpse of the image of Marilyn Monroe. A full-length mirror that once hung in the starlet's favorite suite now hangs in the hallway of the hotel, and guests have reported seeing the image of Marilyn in it. Her ghost has also been spotted at her grave in Westwood Memorial Park and at her house in Brentwood. No comment on the number of times she has been seen alive since her death.

Hollywood is a place where they'll pay you a thousand dollars for a kiss and fifty cents for your soul. I know, because I turned down the first offer often enough and held out for the fifty cents. –MARILYN MONROE

ROCKY MOUNTAIN BYE

Screen siren Carole Lombard was killed on January 16, 1942, when the TWA flight she was on crashed on Table Rock Mountain near Las Vegas. The actress, her mother, and 20 other people were killed. Lombard was returning from a trip to Indianapolis, where she had helped raise more than $2,000,000 in defense bonds.

HAVE GHOST, WILL TRAVEL

Rudolph Valentino's ghost has been spotted in his former bedroom and among the halls of Falcon's Lair, his Beverly Hills mansion, as well as on the porch of his beach house in Oxnard, California. A figure that looks like Valentino in his infamous garb from the movie *The Sheik* (1921) has been reported to walk on a nearby beach. His ghostly image has been seen in the costume department at Paramount Studios, as well as the Santa Maria Inn in Santa Maria, California, and Valentino Place, an apartment complex in Hollywood.

YESTERDREAM

The tune to Paul McCartney's hit song "Yesterday" came to him in a dream. He says of the experience, "I woke up with a lovely tune in my head. I thought, 'That's great. I wonder what that is?' There was an upright piano next to me, to the right of the bed by the window. I got out of bed, sat at the piano, found G, found F sharp minor seventh—and that leads you through then to B to E minor, and finally back to E. It all leads forward logically. I liked the melody a lot; but because I'd dreamed it, I couldn't believe I'd written it. I thought, 'No, I've never written anything like this before.' But I had the tune, which was the most magic thing!"

———— ◄ ► ————

The famous Hollywood sign originally read "Holly-woodland." The letters, constructed in 1923, were originally built to advertise a new housing development in the Hollywood Hills and cost $21,000 to construct. Each letter of the sign was 30 feet wide and 50 feet high, and was illuminated with approximately 4,000 light bulbs. The sign was not intended to be permanent; it was expected to stand only about a year and a half. But after the Los Angeles cinema's rise to popularity, the sign became an internationally recognized symbol, and was thus left in place. It has been refurbished as needed and was eventually rebuilt completely.

FALLEN STAR

Peg Entwistle was a young actress who had found success on the Broadway stage. After her marriage failed and several of her plays flopped during the lean times of the Great Depression, Entwistle made her way to Hollywood to try her luck as a film actress. At the time, directors of the new "talkies," or movies with spoken tracks, were turning to New York–based actors to fill their film roles, as silent film stars were often not sufficiently trained for the parts.

Entwistle landed a short-term contract with RKO Studios and won a small role in the film *Thirteen Women* (1932). What seemed a hopeful success turned out to be a complete flop; the movie itself was received with savage dislike by the critics, and what had been written as a supporting role for Entwistle had been cut to little more than a cameo appearance. After this great disappointment, things turned even worse for the actress. She was dropped by RKO and could no longer find work, not even on stage. Devastated, one night she told her uncle, with whom she lived, that she was going to take a walk. She walked to the site of the now-famous Hollywood sign, climbed up the slope on which it stands, and left her coat, shoes, and purse at the base of the letter H. She then climbed the maintenance ladder leading up the side of the H and jumped to her death. She was just 24.

Her body was found in the 100-foot ravine below two days later, and a suicide note was found in her purse. It read, "I am afraid, I am a coward. I am sorry for everything. If I had done this a long time ago, it would have saved a lot of pain. P. E." The initials and body were identified by her uncle.

Only two days later, her uncle was sifting through the mail when he discovered a letter that had been sent to Entwistle the day before she jumped to her death. It was a note from the Beverly Hills Playhouse stating that they hoped she would play the lead role in their next production. The part they wanted her to play was that of a beautiful young woman who commits suicide at the end of the play.

Since Entwistle's death, there have been many reports of sightings of a pretty blonde woman, dressed in 1930s clothing, who rapidly disappears when approached. Many others have reported smelling gardenias (the actress's signature scent) when no flowers are nearby. A Griffith Park ranger has said that the sign's security system, set up with motion detectors, has at multiple times reported movement not five feet away from him when there is no one else but him standing there.

HARROWING HORROR-MOVIE FACTS

The blood in the infamous shower scene in the film *Psycho* (1960) was actually chocolate syrup.

The Chucky doll, originally seen in *Child's Play* (1988), had the full name of Charles Lee Ray, named after famous killers Charles Manson, Lee Harvey Oswald, and James Earl Ray.

The cult-classic horror film *Alien* (1979) was originally going to be called *Star Beast*.

In *Night of the Living Dead* (1968), the actors playing zombies were paid only one dollar for their work, but each also received a t-shirt that boasted, "I was a zombie in *Night of the Living Dead*."

One of the investors for *Night of the Living Dead* was a butcher who paid the director in blood and intestines from his shop.

Approximately 50 gallons of fake blood were used during the production of *Scream* (1996).

The famous shower scene in *Psycho* took seven days to shoot and involved 77 different shots. Reportedly, Janet Leigh was not told that her character would be murdered during that scene so that she would look genuinely terrified in the shot. Originally, Hitchcock did not want to use the now-famous music played during the murder in the shower, but when he viewed the finished scene with the score, he was so happy with the result that he doubled the salary of the person who suggested the music.

THE EXORCIST:
→→ BEHIND-THE-SCENES CHILLS ←←—

During shooting of *The Exorcist* (1973), director William Friedkin was known to scare his actors into character. He fired a gun before saying "Action" and even slapped actors across the face before their scenes.

When actresses Linda Blair and Ellen Burstyn filmed scenes involving harnesses, he ordered that they both be shaken longer and more brutally than was necessary, injuring both in the process. Burstyn suffered a permanent spinal injury when she was pulled away from her film daughter's bed too quickly and thrown to the floor. The scene during which this injury happened is intact in the movie.

A real priest, the Reverend William O'Malley, played Father Dyer. He was actually involved in the exorcism of a young boy that inspired the movie. He claims that the movie is 80 percent factual.

Originally, Burstyn's character was supposed to say the line, "I believe in the devil," but she agreed to make the film only if the line was removed.

The sound you hear when the demon exits Regan's body is actually a recording of pigs being led to a slaughterhouse.

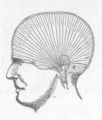

HYSTERICAL BALDNESS

The tortured looks of Shelly Duval in *The Shining* (1980) aren't completely a result of her acting skills: Stanley Kubrick, like his fellow director William Friedkin, put a bit of *method* in the madness, purposely tormenting Duval on set and somehow convincing the rest of the crew to do so as well, to "help" Duval get into the character of a tortured wife and mother. As a result, Duval became sick and lost a lot of hair while filming.

THE CURSE OF THE CROW

Brandon Lee, son of martial arts star Bruce Lee, was a promising young actor when he began work on the 1994 film *The Crow*. On March 31, 1993, he was filming a scene in which his character arrived at home to find his girlfriend being brutally beaten and raped by several thugs. His character was to be shot upon arriving in the apartment. Since filming was already behind schedule, the film's second-unit team made dummy cartridges for the on-set gun by removing gunpowder from real bullets and reinserting the bullets into the gun. What they neglected to consider was that the primer was still live, and therefore, it was still possible for the bullet to emerge from the end of the cartridge. Before the scene was shot, the live primer on one of the constructed dummy rounds was discharged by someone while the bullet was still in the pistol's chamber. The primer provided just enough force to push the bullet out of the cartridge and into the barrel of the revolver.

When actor Michael Massee, playing the murderer of Lee's character, shot the modified gun, the squib load was lodged in the barrel and propelled by the explosion of a low-power, blank cartridge's explosion. It hit Lee in the abdomen and lodged in his spine. Although he was rushed to the hospital and put through a six-hour operation to remove the bullet, Lee was pronounced dead that day.

BEYOND BIZARRE

4. ON THE ROAD: TALES FROM HAUNTED HIGHWAYS AND BYWAYS

GHOSTLY PLANES, TRAINS, AND AUTOMOBILES

Who did you say it was brother?
Who was it fell by the way? I heard the groans of
the dying. But I didn't hear nobody pray.
—ROY ACUFF, *WRECK ON THE HIGHWAY*

WHEN I WAS A GIRL, I DELIGHTED IN WATCHING my mother open the creaking lid to the turn-of-the-century Victrola and carefully place a thick record onto the purple velvet turntable. She turned the crank clockwise, reminding us never to wind it too far. It didn't take long for the scratchy song to begin: "when whiskey and blood run together . . ." Roy Acuff's cautionary tale of the evils of drunk driving and recklessness was a graphic depiction of death on the road. Perhaps it was the haunting memory of this song that inspired me to write this chapter full of horrible accidents, hitchhiker ghosts, train wrecks, bizarre roadside stops, and long, winding drives in the dark of the night, alone in the car on a road so remote no one would hear you scream . . . .

MAN WITHOUT A FACE

The myth of Charlie No-Face, the deformed and ghost-like, yet harmless creature who was said to haunt Pennsylvania country roads, scared teenagers for decades. The man behind the urban legends was Raymond Robinson, a western Pennsylvania boy who was horribly disfigured at eight years old when he climbed on a live electrical line. Robinson barely survived the accident, which rendered his face unrecognizable: he had neither eyes nor a nose, and his mouth was distended and shapeless. He believed that his injuries were so heinous that to expose his face in public would cause mass hysteria, so he stayed indoors, in his childhood home, for most of the rest of his life—except for his nightly walks along nearby country roads. Local gawkers would gather to try and get a glimpse of Robinson, whom they called Charlie No-Face or the Green Man, on one of his walks. Even after his death in 1985, there were several reported sightings of Robinson's ghost ambling alongside the highways.

OFF WITH HIS HEAD!

In late July, 2008, while riding an overnight Greyhound bus through a desolate stretch of Manitoba, Vince Weiguang Li of Edmonton, Alberta, decapitated his seatmate with a hunting knife. While other passengers were dozing in their seats or watching *The Legend of Zorro* (2005) Li started stabbing his seatmate, said Tim McLean, a 22-year-old carnival worker who was listening to music on his headphones. When the bus stopped and other passengers fled, Li cut off McLean's head and waved it at them through the bus window. Traumatized passengers were bused to a hotel in the town of Brandon while police had a standoff with Li. Canadian public safety minister Stockwell Day commented, "The horrific nature of it is probably one of a kind in Canadian history."

CROATIAN TRANSPORTATION

Frane Selak of Croatia has the travel bug—whether fate wills it or not. In 1962, he survived a train crash that killed 17 passengers when it plunged into a freezing river. In 1963, he was traveling by plane when the door blew away from the cockpit. Nineteen passengers were killed, but Selak landed in a haystack, safe and sound. Between 1966 and 1996, he survived a bus crash, two car crashes in which his car exploded in flames, getting hit by a city bus, and driving off a cliff to escape an oncoming truck (he landed in a tree). But Selak doesn't mind: in 2003 he won $1,000,000 dollars in the Croatian lottery.

The engine with
murderous blood was damp
And was brilliantly lit
with a brimstone lamp;
An imp, for fuel,
was shoveling bones,
While the furnace rang
with a thousand groans.
The boiler was filled
with lager beer
And the devil himself
was the engineer . . .
—UNKNOWN, "THE HELL-BOUND TRAIN"

STUPID, DUMB, HYPHY, AND DEAD!

"Ghost-riding the whip" is a stunt in which a driver blasts hyphy (a style of hip-hop characterized by manic, exuberant silliness), shifts the car into neutral, slides out the window, and dances on the hood of the still-moving car. It's called ghost-riding because there's nobody behind the wheel. Many would-be ghost riders have sustained injuries or damaged their cars when attempting the stunt. At least two people have died: one 18 year old who hit his head on a parked car, and one 36-year-old man who fell off a moving car. Who's a ghost *now?*

HAUNTED 365

One rainy night, a man driving along Highway 365 in central Arkansas picked up a young girl in a white dress. She directed him to a home in Redfield. When they got there, the man went around the car to open the passenger door and found that the girl had disappeared. Bewildered, the man went up to the house to inquire about the girl. The man who answered the door told him that his daughter had been killed on that very night four years ago.

TRANSPORTATION FAIL

Planes taking off from the Gibraltar Airport require a couple additional air-traffic-control specialists—or, should we say, land-traffic-control specialists? The airport's runway happens to intersect with the city's main north-south artery, Winston Churchill Avenue. Every time a plane departs from the airport, road traffic must be completely shut down.

NOW THAT'S DRUNK

A 21-year-old man in Santa Fe, New Mexico was arrested after a harrowing police chase that resulted in the man running over his own legs. In November of 2008, the man was followed by a state police officer on suspicion of drunk driving. The man refused to pull over, and the officer pursued him as he narrowly avoided several collisions with other vehicles. He finally drove his truck into a ditch and through a barbed-wire fence. When the man left the vehicle, he mistakenly put it into reverse instead of park, and he subsequently fell out of the driver's side and into the path of his front tires. His truck drove over his legs. He was arrested after being treated for minor injuries at the local hospital.

CAVE INN

The Oregon Caves Chateau, built in 1934, is home to the legend of a poltergeist. The innkeepers say that a woman named Elizabeth killed herself sometime after 1937 and now haunts the third floor of the inn. Employees say that it is not unusual for neatly folded laundry to become inexplicably unfolded, faucets to turn on and off on their own, and the grand piano in the lobby to play itself. Should you wish to visit or dare to stay the night, rooms 309 and 310 are reported to be the most haunted. You can find the Oregon Caves Chateau in the Oregon Caves National Park, off of Highway 46, near Cave Junction in southwestern Oregon.

We're on a ride to nowhere,
come on inside
Taking that ride to nowhere,
we'll take that ride.
—TALKING HEADS, "ROAD TO NOWHERE"

HERE'S JOHNNY . . .

If you find yourself traveling in the Denver area, you may want to take a delightfully frightful jaunt into the nearby Rocky Mountain National Park. Among the many sights and sounds (spooky and serene) of this beautiful park, you will find one of the most haunted hotels in America—the Stanley Hotel in Estes Park. The Stanley Hotel is most widely known for inspiring Stephen King's horror novel *The Shining*. Although the infamous movie starring Jack Nicholson was not filmed here, the Stanley Hotel is said to be home to several ghosts. Rooms 407, 217, 401, and 418 are all reported to be haunted by a variety of spirits.

If the Stanley Hotel is fully booked, you can try the nearby Baldplate Inn, which is reputed to be haunted by its original owner, Ethel Mace. An outspoken prohibitionist in life, Mace's ghost has been known to send cocktails flying off tables.

TOW TAG

In March of 2010, the NY *Daily News* reported that a police tow truck towed a minivan parked outside Redden's Funeral Home. The van, whose identifying placard had fallen from the window, happened to contain a dead body! The vehicle was towed to the impound, from which the distraught funeral home owner retrieved it. He managed to get the body on the flight to its intended funeral destination.

I want to travel the common road
With the great crowd surging by,
Where there's many a laugh
and many a load,
And many a smile and sigh.
—SILAS H. PERKINS, "THE COMMON ROAD"

DID YOU EVER THINK?

The word *hearse* has taken several linguistic turns from its origins in 51 BC to its use in 16th century England through modern times. In ancient Rome, a farmer would plow his fields and then use a tool known as a *hirpex* to rake the land. Conquering western Europe, the Romans introduced this agricultural tool to their new subjects, and the tool became commonly called a *harrow* in the British Isles. When the Normans invaded England, they called the harrow a *herse*. They also began the practice of inverting the herse, as it bore resemblance to their own ecclesiastical candelabra. In time, all church candelabras became known as herses, and they grew in size. The candelabras were a common part of a funeral ceremony, beginning the association of a herse with a funeral. In time, the herse itself rested on the coffin lid, and eventually rode on the coffin as the funeral procession made its way to the burial grounds. (The funeral procession needed to move slowly, lest the herse's candles blow out, and the tradition of slow-moving funeral processions continues today.) By the next century, the entire cart that carried the coffin became known as the *hearse*.

"BUT MARGE, I WANT TO GO TO THE CHILI COOK-OFF!"

A funeral parlor in Pittsfield, Massachusetts goes to great lengths to keep business alive. The Devanny-Condron Funeral Home hopes that events such as a chili cook-off, a murder mystery show, an art walk, and monthly birthday cakes at the Pittsfield Senior Center will serve as a reminder to folks that they are an important part of the community.

MMMMM . . . DONUTS

What suits a road trip better than a box of delicious donuts?

The West Coast is host to more than one trendy and morbid donut shop. In Portland, Oregon, the now-infamous Voodoo Donuts features outrageous combinations and sumptuous specialties—including its namesake: a voodoo-doll donut. With two locations, the shop's ever-evolving donut menu includes bacon-maple bars and donuts topped with your favorite childhood cereals: Lucky Charms, Coco Puffs, Captain Crunch . . . and if that isn't enough, you can ask for just about anything on your donut as a special order for parties! You can also order a coffin full of donuts. Visit Voodoo's website to see pics of the donuts, and check out their special events, which include donut-eating contests. Voodoo is open 24 hours, and they perform weddings at both locations, which can include coffee and donuts for your guests.

CRYBABY BRIDGE

Ohio is a pretty unassuming state, but it has an inordinate amount of what are called crybaby bridges—bridges that have had live babies thrown over them. The circumstances behind each incident are pretty much the same: a young woman has been able to hide her pregnancy, but when her child is born, she throws it over a bridge to fend for itself in the murky deep. It is said that if you turn off your car engine on one of Ohio's crybaby bridges, you can hear the wails of a newborn child in the wind.

MAKE MINE A GREYHOUND

On August 2008, in Sunnydale, California, traffic was slowed to a crawl on Highway 101 due to an overturned big rig that was transporting vodka. California Department of Transportation (Caltrans) crews were on the scene to soak up the booze with an absorbent. Although residents were hopeful, there was no word of a truckload of oranges crashing.

THE HAUNTING OF FLIGHT 401

Between 1973 and 1974 on board numerous Eastern Airlines L-1011 jets, passengers and crew reported seeing, hearing, and even speaking to apparitions of Captain Bob Loft and Second Officer Don Repo. The ghostly crew members were both victims of the crash of Eastern Airlines flight 401—which had gone down into the Florida Everglades on December 29th, 1972. Passengers on separate flights correctly identified the deceased crew members, and flight engineers, pilots, and flight attendants all verified similar encounters with the ghosts of Loft and Repo. The crash and the reported sightings became the subject for *The Ghosts of Flight 401*, a book written by John G. Fuller in 1983.

BLOOD ALLEY

There is a winding road that runs between Wickenburg and Kingman, Arizona with so many accident-causing blind curves that it's earned the name Blood Alley. Blood Alley is a dead zone, meaning no cell phone reception, and often radios don't work either. The road is dotted with crosses alongside its narrow two lanes to mark the many victims who have died along this pass.

Many passers of this roadway have reported ghoulish encounters with the souls of those who have perished along its twists and turns.

SUNSHINE ON MY SHOULDERS MAKES ME SCARED

In 1980, four shipping accidents and fifty deaths in fewer than five months was enough to start rumors that the Sunshine Bridge at Tampa Bay, Florida, was cursed.

THE GHOST OF THE BAY BRIDGE

Countless commuters have seen the figure of a man, usually dressed in a 1940s-era hat and coat, just after the Yerba Buena Island tunnel when heading westbound (into San Francisco) on the San Francisco–Oakland Bay Bridge. Speculation about the shadowy figure points to a man who died in an accident on the bridge during the mid-1940s.

SOAP ON A ROPE

Mount Olympus, Washington, is home to Lake Crescent, a pristine mountain lake that is more than 600 feet deep in spots. Native to the region, the Kallam Indians would not fish the waters of this lake for fear of stirring up evil spirits that lurked beneath the glassy surface. There is also a haunting tale of what locals call "the Lady of the Lake."

Hallie Illingworth's body was discovered by two fishermen in 1940. The young lady worked as a waitress at the nearby Crescent Lake Lodge and had gone missing some three years earlier. It turned out that her husband had killed her, wrapped her in blankets, and tied stones to her body with heavy rope. He threw her weighted body into the lake, presumably never to be discovered again. Illingworth's body was remarkably well preserved, thanks to the cold waters of the lake causing a process known as "saponification," which causes the flesh to be rendered into something quite soaplike.

Lake Crescent is also to the site of numerous accounts of Bigfoot or Sasquatch sightings, as well as accounts of ghosts and ghostly sounds in the woods. You can hike this fantastically frightening stretch of the Pacific Northwest by taking the Spruce Railroad Trail in the Olympic National Park.

WANDERING JACK

The origins of the jack-o'-lantern are told in a popular Irish folk tale. A man named Jack chased the devil into a tree, then drew a cross on its trunk so the devil couldn't get down. Pleased with himself, Jack walked away, back to his rather unseemly life of greed and sloth. When Jack died, he was denied access to heaven for being sinful. And the devil, who had eventually managed to get out of that tree, wouldn't let Jack into hell, either. Jack was doomed to walk the earth forever.

The devil, in a rare sympathetic mood, felt pity for Jack and gave him some burning coal to light his way. Jack was eating a turnip at the time. He took one bite, decided he would rather go hungry, and put the burning coal inside the turnip. And that was the first jack-'o-lantern ever made. When Halloween came to the United States, people started making their jack-o'-lanterns out of pumpkins.

5. BLOOD-RED CROSSES AND GROSS ANATOMY: HOSPITAL HORRORS

BIZARRE DISEASES AND MALADIES,
HAUNTED HOSPITALS AND ASYLUMS,
EVIL DOCTORS, STRANGE PROCEDURES,
AND VERY GRAVE ROBBERIES

I am convinced that of all quackeries,
the physician's is the grotesquest and the silliest.

—MARK TWAIN

I DON'T KNOW MANY PEOPLE WHO WOULD declare, "I love hospitals!" For those of us who don't work in the medical field, a trip to the doctor's often causes at least a tinge of dread. This chapter won't make you feel any better—consider the use of maggots in modern medical practice, or the ancient condition known as lousy disease. From the fascinating to the grotesque, nothing illustrates the marvel of the human body like a woman who lives with a worm in her head, or a 61-year-old grandmother giving birth to her own grandchild. And nothing says horrifying like tales of grave robbery and human experimentation. Warning: this chapter made even *my* flesh crawl!

REGULATION PROCEDURE

The National Alliance on Mental Illness (NAMI) is fighting to make the public aware of the gross misrepresentation of mental patients during the Halloween holidays. Every year, the organization's email campaign alerts people of the stigmas they perpetuate when they use "funny farm" and "loony bin" themes for parties, haunted houses, and costumes. They also crusade against year-round infractions, such as the Crazy for You teddy bear, which was released in 2005 and featured stuffed bear in a straight jacket, and careless statements, such as one made by *Grey's Anatomy* and *Private Practice* actress Kate Walsh, who was quoted in 2007 as saying she likes spending her weekend in men's flannel pajamas, "like a mental patient."

HOSPITAL FOOD AIN'T THAT BAD

In 2009, a new theme restaurant opened in Riga, Latvia. Called "Hospitals," it is owned by a group of doctors, features nurses as waitresses, food on gurneys, beakers filled with drinks, and a dining room designed to look like an operating room. There is even a cake with edible fingers, noses, and tongues for dessert.

The fingernails on your dominant hand grow faster than the fingernails on your nondominant hand.

MAGGOT ACT

The U.S. Food and Drug Administration (FDA) approved maggots as a medical device in January 2004. Placed in a wound, maggots eat the dead flesh. After several days, they leave the wound in search of a dry place to become pupae. But not just any maggot larvae can be used in the United States. FDA regulations say you must get a prescription from your doctor for sterilized maggot larvae.

The use of maggots in medicine has a long history. One of Napoleon's surgeons wrote an account of soldiers with maggot-infested wounds healing faster than those whose wounds were wriggle free.

THAT'S WHAT THEY CALL IT?

Frotteurism: Rubbing up against people without their consent. This condition is most commonly diagnosed in males between the ages of 15 and 25. The guy rubs his gentalia against an unsuspecting victim's thighs or fondles the victim.

> Nothing is less reliable than [a machine] . . . [I]t is difficult not to wonder whether that combination of elements which produces a machine for labor does not create also a soul of sorts, a dull resentful metallic will, which can rebel at times. —PEARL S. BUCK, *MY SEVERAL WORLDS*

Nicotine dependence is considered a psychiatric illness.

ONE-EYED WILLY

The first human organ transplant took place in Moravia (Czech Republic) on December 7, 1905, and was performed by the Austrian surgeon Eduard Zirm. He transplanted the corneas of an 11-year-old boy onto the eyes of a laborer who had been blinded. One cornea took, but the other transplant was rejected.

The sweatiest part of the human body is not the armpits, but the palms of the hands.

GROSS BUT TRUE

Doctors use cockroaches to study heart disease and cancer. Apparently, cockroaches grow tumors not unlike human tumors, and the nerve cells in their brains are similar to those of humans.

WORMING YOUR WAY IN

Imagine the mixture of horror and relief you would feel upon discovering that what you thought was a life-threatening tumor in your brain was, in fact, a worm! A woman in Arizona was experiencing classic symptoms of a brain tumor, including blurred vision and numbness in her arm. After two emergency room visits and a clear CAT scan, doctors were stumped. When doctors took a closer look at an MRI, they noticed something deep down in her brain stem. The woman was scheduled for surgery immediately, and doctors began the procedure to remove what they thought would be a tumor. Instead, they were shocked to find a worm. Surgeons removed the worm from her brain, and the woman made a full recovery. Doctors say that many conditions, such as eating uncooked pork or not washing your hands properly after using the bathroom, can lead to worms entering your internal system.

LET THERE BE SIGHT

After three years of near-total blindness, a 90-year-old Oregon man's sight was unexpectedly restored in 2009. After calling 911 because he was feeling faint, Marty

Alvey was taken to the hospital. He began to feel better en route, and by the time the doctor came to his room, his vision had been restored. Two ophthalmologists examined his eyes and found no explanation for the remarkable improvement.

GLOW-IN-THE-DARK HUMANS

In July 2009, Japanese scientists revealed their findings that the human body emits a glow. This light is visible, but faint, and its levels rise and fall throughout the day. The scientists used sensitive cameras to photograph a cross-section of five men in their twenties. Recording their findings, they found that the body's lowest light levels occur around 10 a.m. and the highest at 4 a.m., and faces glowed more than the rest of the body.

If it's true that every seven years each cell in your body dies and is replaced, then I have truly inherited my life from a dead man; and the misdeeds of those times have been forgiven, and are buried with his bones.
—NEIL GAIMAN

ONE-FOOT BRAIN

In a remarkable 2008 story from Colorado Springs, Colorado, a fully developed infant foot was discovered in the brain of a newborn baby who was being operated on for a life-threatening tumor. Doctors explained that it is not uncommon for the type of tumor presented to be tissue—most often muscle, hair, or teeth—from an undeveloped fetal twin. It is extremely rare for the tissue to develop this far. The foot was removed, and the infant was expected to make a full recovery.

SIX FEET LOWER THAN MOST

In 2008, in Philadelphia, Pennsylvania, Louis and Gerald Garzone, two brothers who owned and operated a funeral home, were found guilty of selling corpses to a black-market trafficker of body parts. The gruesome duo admitted to carving up nearly 250 bodies without family permission and selling the body parts across the country for various purposes, including dental implants, hip and knee replacements, and other medical procedures.

In an elaborate and grisly scheme, the brothers would sell the bodies or body parts to Michael Mastromarino, who ran the company Biomedical Tissue Services. Mastromarino would collect bodies from several funeral homes in the New York and New Jersey area. He would send a crew to cut up the bodies and then transport the parts to various biomedical facilities—at a hefty price. Tissue from a single body could be sold for as much as $4,000.

The selling of bodies for medical purposes itself is not illegal, provided the family and/or the deceased have consented, and the body has been tested and certified to be free of disease. Most of the bodies sold by the Garzones and Mastromarino were given false names and documentation, received no medical testing, and in some cases, had not been stored or refrigerated properly.

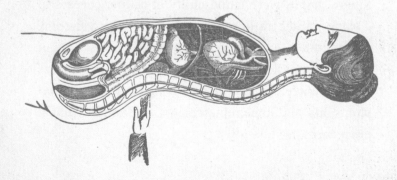

LOUSY DISEASE

Phthiriasis, or the lousy disease, is a malady in which tumors or eruptions of the skin, when sliced or burst open, are found to teem with lice. The disease dates back to ancient times. Aristotle described it in his *History of Animals,* and there are many accounts dating back to the 2nd century BC. It was widely believed that this disease was divine punishment.

While numerous famous cases of this horrifying infestation exist in literature and medical records, its actual existence was the subject of extensive medical debate. Many doctors and scientists offered evidence to disprove the disease, claiming that it was impossible for lice to erupt under the skin in such a fashion. One of the lousy disease's distinguishing characteristics was the lack of pus or fluid; the infestations were dry and would produce eruptions only of lice. It was well known by the 1800s that lice and other small creatures could and did infest unclean areas or infected wounds, but the idea that lice could produce the lumps themselves was laughed at as a legend, akin to dragons, by many medical professionals of the 19th century.

However, modern archaeologists have proven the existence of a kind of mite that produces tumors on birds. When sliced apart, the lumps spill forth no fluids, but rather hundreds of the tiny, wriggling bodies of the mites.

Lateral epicondylitis is the medical term for tennis elbow.

Famous composer Frédéric Chopin is beloved even in death. His heart, preserved with alcohol, is kept in a jar at Warsaw's Holy Cross Church, sealed inside a pillar. It has been there since the Polish composer's death in

1849, save for being removed once to protect it during World War II. In 2008, scientists requested permission to test the heart, believing that Chopin died of cystic fibrosis, thought his death certificate gives his cause of death as tuberculosis. But the National Frédéric Chopin Institute was not convinced that there was cause enough to disturb the musical mastermind's remains. Chopin's heart is considered one of Poland's greatest treasures. Although he died in France, he had requested that his heart be sent to his homeland.

LIKE MOTHER, LIKE DAUGHTER

In Tokyo, Japan, in 2007, a 61-year-old woman gave birth to her own grandchild. The woman served as a surrogate for her daughter, whose eggs were viable, but who had no uterus. The Suwa Maternity Clinic, in Japan, has had a total of eight surrogate mothers give birth. Of those eight, four of them used fertilized eggs from their own daughters.

According to *The Century Book of Facts* published in the year 1900, there were 106,485 insane people in the United States. Of these, 53,473 were male and 53,012 were female.

EAT THIS, NOT THAT

At the turn of the century, the following antidotes were recommended for specific poisons:

Arsenic: A prompt emetic of one tablespoon mustard and one tablespoon salt in a cup of warm water, followed by sweet oil, warm butter, or milk.

Alcohol: First give an emetic, then dash head with cold water and give ammonia (spirits of hartshorn).

Belladonna: An emetic of mustard, salt, and water followed by vinegar and water or lemonade.

Tobacco: Emetics, frequent draughts of cold water; also camphor and brandy.

MEDICAL MALADIES

Achalasia is the inability to relax the muscles of a hollow organ.

Agnosia is the inability to recognize persons, things, or information conveyed by any of the five senses.

A creeping eruption is a skin disorder caused by larvae burrowing under the skin, producing red lines that seem to move forward at one end and fade at the other as the larvae migrate under the skin.

Diplegia is the paralysis of corresponding parts on both sides of the body.

Macrognathia is the term for having long jaws.

Marfan's syndrome is a combination of special physical characteristics: abnormally long "spider" fingers, unusually flexible joints, and a partially dislocated lens of the eye.

Ottorrhea is discharge from the ear, especially pus-containing discharge.

Raynaud's disease is a condition in which the arteries supplying blood to the fingers and toes become temporarily narrowed, reducing the blood flow; the extremities first become white, then purple and painful. This disease is sometimes caused by cold.

Syringobulbia is a chronic disease characterized by cavities in the brain stem, which interfere with automatic activities of the brain, such as breathing.

Taenia saginata, also known as the beef tapeworm, is a ribbonlike flatworm usually found in undercooked meat. When ingested by the human body, the worm does not always cause symptoms, and even when it does, the symptoms are often mild, such as abdominal complaints. When flushed from the body, the worm's head must be removed, lest it reattach itself to the intestinal wall and begin to grow again.

Weil's disease is a severe illness caused by infection with spirochetes. It is spread by rats. It causes jaundice and also affects the kidneys.

BIRTH OF THE BAND-AID

In the 1920s, Earle Dickson worked for the Johnson & Johnson Company. He was also recently married to a woman who had a knack for cutting herself while doing housework. Time and time again, Dickson brought her gauze and tape, but the rigorous nature of keeping house caused the bandage to fall off. Dickson folded the gauze into a narrow pad, unrolled the tape, laid gauze over it, and placed a band of crinoline over the whole thing to keep the tape from sticking to itself. When he mentioned this endeavor to his co-workers, the Band-Aid was born.

Paleopathology is the study of the ancient evidences of disease.

INVASION OF THE BODY SNATCHERS

In his 1929 book *Devils, Drugs, and Doctors,* Dr. Howard Haggard tells tales of body snatching, human experimentation, and murder. The following is one of Haggard's terrifyingly true tales.

In 1827, in Edinburgh, William Hare and William Burke struck up a most morbid partnership. They committed a series of murders in order to obtain bodies for dissection. Hare and Burke and their female companions all lived in a boarding house run by Hare. The majority of its tenants were poor and downtrodden. When an old man who boarded there died, the parish sent a coffin into which the body was supposedly placed. But Hare and Burke had secretly removed the coffin lid, stolen the corpse, refilled the coffin with tanner's bark, and replaced the lid. They sold the body to one Dr. Knox for seven pounds and ten shillings. This was the first of what would be many crimes, including 16 murders, committed by the gruesome twosome. In another evil act, the pair enticed an old pauper woman into the house, plying her with alcohol until she passed out, and then suffocating her.

The two managed to get away with this illicit trade for a number of years, primarily because they killed paupers and castaways, people whose disappearances society took little notice of. But two of their last victims did not quite fit the profile. One was young Mary Paterson, whose reputation was unsavory, but widely known. And the other, James Wilson, who was commonly called Daft Jamie. Though he lived on the streets in Edinburgh, his good nature led him to be a familiar figure. The disappearances of both of these characters, along that of with another woman, led to a search that eventually resulted in the arrest of Hare, Burke, and Helen McDougal, Hare's mistress. Burke was hanged in a public square on January 27, 1829. Hare turned over evidence to the state and McDougal was released.

In the 1500s, cautery was common means of controlling hemorrhaging. Boiling oil, molten pitch, or red-hot irons were poured on a wound to staunch bleeding. The pain and additional injury caused by this procedure made wounds heal slowly. French surgeon Ambroise Paré (1510–1590) used a method of tying the ends of severed blood vessels with cords, an early version of what surgeons do today.

PILE HIGH CLUB

During the mid-14th century, at the height of the bubonic plague outbreak in Europe, bodies were often buried together in large graves, sometimes resulting in the graveyard becoming a foot or more taller than its original height.

The world's first face transplant took place in 2005. Isabelle Dinoire of Valenciennes, France, received a new face to replace the nose, lips, and chin that had been severely injured when she was attacked by a dog.

BACK FROM THE DEAD

On January 7, 1942, Dr. Herbert D. Adams and Dr. Leo V. Hand of Boston reported in the *Journal of the American Medical Association* that they were able to revive a man who had been dead for 20 minutes. The patient's heart had stopped beating during a lung operation, and the doctors successfully brought him back to life by keeping his brain and the rest of his body supplied with oxygen and artificially manipulating his heart's rhythm.

Onychomancy is divination by fingernails.

NOW FEAR THIS

Aichmophobia: **fear of needles**

Arachibutyrophobia: **fear of peanut butter sticking to the roof of one's mouth**

Cremnophobia: **fear of precipices**

Erythrophobia: **fear of blushing**

Lyssophobia: **fear of going insane**

Nosophobia: **fear of disease**

Peccatophobia: **fear of sinning**

Sesquipedalophobia: **fear of long words**

NOSE WAY

Ever wondered why some people sneeze when they're exposed to bright light? Me neither. But this honest-to-god phenomenon, called photic sneeze reflex, is a genetic trait that causes some people to sneeze, sometimes continuously, when they're in bright light. The condition apparently affects 18 to 25 percent of the population!

According to the 2006 Old Spice "Sweatiest City in America" study, Phoenix, Arizona has the most perspirers. The average resident sweats 26 ounces per hour.

MOM'S GOT MUSCLE

While not a recognized medical condition, hysterical strength is characterized by the demonstration of superhuman strength, usually brought on by some emergency situation. One reported occurrence took place in Lawrenceville, Georgia, when a mother lifted up the body of a car to free her son, who had been working underneath it when it fell on him.

Hemicorporectomy is a drastic surgical procedure that removes the entire body below the waist, including the legs, genitalia, pelvis, anus, and rectum. It is recommended only as a last resort for patients with aggressive infections, tumors, or trauma, and has been recorded only a couple dozen times in medical literature.

GO EAT DIRT!

The technical term for eating dirt is *geophagia*. There are pockets of Georgia and Alabama where people eat a type of white clay called kaolin. Pregnant women are said to crave it, and it's sold in rural grocery stores. A one-pound bag costs only $1.49.

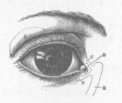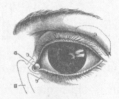

I SWEAR, I'M SHOCKED

People born with Moebius syndrome cannot make facial expressions; they can't smile, frown, or make a barfing face when they smell what's cooking for dinner. They are often found sleeping with their eyes open.

The invention of the stethoscope was the result of one man's prudishness. He was examining a patient with a heart defect, and was unable to listen to her heart in the traditional way—by thumping his hand on her back and listening to the sound it made—because she was too portly. Embarrassed to lay his ear against her ample bosom, the doctor created a do-it-yourself stethoscope out of a rolled-up piece of paper. He later refined his design to invent what we know as the stethoscope.

Studies show that our bodies deteriorate a lot more slowly than they did 50 years ago. It seems that we eat so much processed food these days that our bodies take longer to break it all down.

ARE YOU GOING TO EAT THAT?

Do you crave pencils for lunch and soap for dinner? You might be suffering from pica, a disorder characterized by the persistent desire to eat nonfood items. The word comes from the Latin term for "magpie" and frequently occurs in people with autism and developmental disorders, although it can happen to people without those disorders as well. Common cravings? Clay, plaster, laundry starch, buttons, cigarette butts, and coffee grounds.

ONLY IN LAS VEGAS

In Las Vegas, gambling doesn't stop at the casino! In 1980, several workers were suspended from a hospital in Las Vegas for betting on when patients would die.

THE GHOSTS OF "HELL"

Northampton State Hospital, in Northampton, Massachusetts, was home to thousands of mentally ill people over the course of its 200-year history. Nicknamed "Hell" by patients' relatives, the establishment was closed in the mid-1990s. But visitors to the site's buildings can still hear the squeak of a ghostly wheelchair coming down the hall, doors slamming for no apparent reason, and disembodied footsteps.

THE SWINGING CURE

Doctors in the 19th century had some pretty innovative ideas about treating mental illness. Asylums in England used to strap patients into a rotating machine that would whirl them around the room at high speeds. The motion of the ride was supposed to calm the patient's nerves.

ONE LONG PREGNANCY

Two hundred and ninety cases of lithopedions have been reported in the medical literature. A lithopedion, often called a "stone child," is the calcefied remains of an extrauterine pregnancy. A pregnant woman might carry a lithopedion for decades before getting it removed. Lithopedions have been discovered in women as old as 100.

ALPHABET SOUP

The brain is the most complex organ in the body, filled with thousands of nerve fibers that, like electrical cables, can become crossed or rewired. Some people, such as those with synesthesia, are born with unusual brain wirings. Synesthesia is a neurological condition in which something perceived by one of the body's five senses simultaneously triggers sensations in another of the senses. Richard Murray, for example, is a U.K. man whose extreme case of synesthesia causes him to taste distinct flavors when he hears words said aloud. Different words evoke different flavors: the Lord's Prayer fills his mouth with the taste of bacon, while the name *Colleen* makes him feel sick. When he was a child, Murray claims, he chose his friends based on the flavors he associated with their names. Now he mostly eats dinner alone so he can fully appreciate the *real* flavors of his food and works at a quiet desk job so he's not constantly stimulated by taste sensations.

BLOOD NOT-SO-SIMPLE

Even broken down into its simplest parts, blood is a pretty complex substance. Vampires drink it, humanitarians donate it, and just the thought of it makes some people faint. It makes up seven percent of our body weight, and it's the stuff that keeps us alive. So it's not surprising that the sticky substance is the subject of much speculation, myth, fable, and folklore, as well as good old-fashioned fact. Here's a brief sampling of blood-related oddities:

- If someone were to literally rip your heart out and place it on the end of a long-jump track, the powerful pressure of its pumping mechanism would squirt blood upwards of 30 feet.

- The average life span of a red blood cell is 120 days.

- A newborn baby has about one cup of blood in his body.

- There are approximately 100,000 miles of blood vessels in the human body.

> In the early 19th century, some advertisements claimed that riding a carousel was good for the circulation of blood.

CHRISTMAS MIRACLE

When Tracy Hermanstorfer of Colorado went into labor on the morning of December 24, 2009, no one could anticipate the drama that was to come. With her husband Mike by her side, Tracy was being prepped for childbirth when she suddenly felt sleepy. She stopped breathing, and her heart stopped. Doctors were unable to revive her. They made the decision to deliver her baby by Cesarean, and when the child was removed from her womb, he too appeared lifeless. While his father held him, the doctors successfully resuscitated him. Tracy, meanwhile, continued to have no heartbeat for four minutes. Yet as she was being wheeled from the room for emergency surgery, her pulse returned. A Christmas miracle? Mike Hermanstorfer sure thinks so.

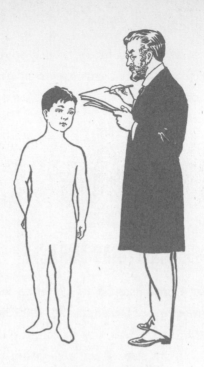

BLOOD RELATION

If you've ever seen a hippopotamus basking under a hot sun, you probably wondered what the sticky, oily, blood-colored substance secreting out of its pores is. The ancient Greeks thought the hippo's skin was so sensitive that it bled when exposed to the sun's rays. But according to a team of Japanese scientists, the "blood" is actually the mammals' sweat, which also works as sunscreen and protects the hippo from harmful pathogens.

Blood-spatter specialists use a combination of biology, chemistry, mathematics, and physics to analyze the circumstances of a crime, including what object was used to commit the crime and where the victim and perpetrator were physically located when the former's blood was shed.

The vampire bat is a heavy drinker, consuming more than its body weight in blood each night.

The ancient Greeks believed that the blood of the gods, which they called ichor, was poisonous to mortals.

Humans suffering from *sulfhemoglobinemia* ooze blue or greenish blood.

6. MURDER, SHE WROTE

TRUE CRIME AND UNSOLVED MYSTERIES

My loathings are simple: stupidity,
oppression, crime, cruelty, soft music.
—VLADIMIR NABAKOV

A MYSTERY LEFT UNSOLVED. A COUPLE
murdered inside their own tent. A ghost revealing the
name of her own murderer. There is nothing more terrifying than the pure evil that lurks inside the brain of
a killer—except for meeting that killer in a dark alley
somewhere. These stories of unspeakable crimes, psychic mystery solvers, and ghostly visitors are sure to
infuse a little terror into the minds of even the bravest
true crime connoisseurs.

More serial killers come from the United States than from any other country.

SINISTER SERIAL KILLERS: JERRY BRUDOS

The detail that makes serial killer Jerry Brudos's murders so chilling is that many of them took place in his own garage, under the noses of his wife and children. Brudos, a tall, porky man dubbed the Lust Killer, was gaining a reputation as a nuisance to female students at Oregon State University in the summer of 1969. Police contacted a sympathetic woman who had agreed to go on a date with Brudos, who had told her he was a lonely Vietnam veteran just looking to talk. When he called the woman for a second date, she alerted the authorities, and Brudos was brought in for questioning. Though he seemed suspicious, the police had nothing to charge him with, and he was released. But he remained under surveillance.

Just days later, the police had enough evidence to arrest Brudos: a girl who had recently been the victim of an attempted kidnapping identified his face out of a photo spread. Once under custody, Brudos confessed freely, even gleefully: between 1968 and April 1969, he had murdered four women and had sex with their corpses, keeping parts of their bodies as souvenirs. His first victim, a young encyclopedia saleswoman, had followed him into his workshop. Brudos hit her over the head with a piece of wood, killing her. Calmly and methodically, he got his wife, children, and mother to leave the house, cut up the girl's body, and began the work of disposing of it. He kept one token to remember her by: her foot.

Brudos confessed to the murders of three other girls and offered up some disturbing details about his workshop of death. He had installed a hook and pulley system in the ceiling, with which he was able to haul the girls' bodies into the air—often to take photographs of them dressed in various outfits. At some point he purchased a large freezer for storing body parts.

Brudos's crimes were truly grisly, and he was punished for them: in 1970, he received three consecutive life sentences for the murders of three girls. He died in prison in 2006.

Frightening fact: The ice-truck killer portrayed in the TV show *Dexter* is modeled after Jerry Brudos.

NO ONE COULD HAVE PREDICTED THIS

CNN reported in 2009 that psychics are one of a few groups to have actually *benefited* from the economic crisis of 2008. One psychic told reporters that her clientele had grown significantly and expanded to include lots of different types of people, from businessmen to housewives. It seems that the downturn has prompted even the most logical, type-A-personality folks to seek guidance from "untraditional" sources.

Dreaming. Either one does not dream at all, or one dreams in an interesting manner. One must learn to be awake in the same fashion: either not at all, or in an interesting manner. —FRIEDRICH NIETZSCHE

BASA'S GHOST

The murder of Filipina physical therapist Teresita Basa was merciless: the 48-year-old daughter of a prominent judge was strangled, stabbed through the heart, and burned to death in her apartment. Details surrounding the murder were scarce, but she apparently knew her killer; she was on the phone with a friend when the killer knocked on the door and was let inside her apartment.

About two weeks after Basa's murder, Remy Chua, a co-worker at the hospital where she had been employed, offhandedly joked to a colleague that Basa should come to her in a dream to reveal her killer. Later, Chua took a nap. She opened her eyes to see the image of Basa standing before her, solid as a living person.

Over the next couple weeks, Chua's family noticed that she was acting strangely. Normally carefree and cheerful, she was moody and reserved, as Basa had been. She even began to resemble Basa.

One night, Chua's husband heard his wife talking in her sleep. She was repeating "Al—Al—Al" and sounded distressed. She later told him that she had dreamt that she was inside a smoky room. The next day Chua felt extremely ill, and her parents came to her house to look after her. In the middle of her fevered sleep, Chua started babbling in Spanish—a language she didn't know. When her husband asked her how she felt, she replied, "I am Teresita Basa. I want help . . . Nothing has been done about the man who killed me." With that, Chua woke up, herself again.

Days later, Chua felt a pain in her chest. "Terrie is here again," she told her mother. Then the voice of Teresita Basa spoke through her, saying, "Allan killed me. I let Al into the apartment, and he killed me. Al came to fix my television, and he killed me and burned me. Tell the police. The man Allan Showery stole my jewelry and gave it to his girlfriend." Chua, still speaking in Basa's voice, went on to tell her husband who would be able to identify the stolen jewelry, even providing a phone number.

Chua's family, understandably shaken by her possession, didn't know what to do immediately. Eventually, her father phoned the police and explained the whole story. When the police checked up on Showery, they found that he had a long criminal record that included two rapes. He was brought to the police station, where he admitted to entering Basa's apartment on the night of the murder, but denied killing her. But when Showery's girlfriend arrived wearing the new ring her boyfriend had given her, the jig was up. It was identified as Basa's ring, and Showery was brought to trial for her murder.

On September 9, 2009 (9/9/09), an Arkansas couple welcomed their baby girl into the world. The same couple had had another daughter the year before—on August 8, 2008 (8/8/08)!

MURDER, SHE WROTE

Seventeen-year-old Kemi Adeyoola was the privileged daughter of London millionaires. She had big plans to become a millionaire herself, but not through conventional means. When she was sent to juvenile hall for shoplifting, she drafted a 20-page plan outlining how to make 3 million pounds by killing and robbing elderly ladies. When the document was discovered during a room search, Adeyoola claimed it was the outline of a crime novel she planned to write. But after she was released from prison in 2005, she snuck into her 84-year-old neighbor's house, cut the telephone lines, and stabbed the woman 14 times. After being caught and tried, she was sentenced to life in prison.

I WILL NEVER GO CAMPING AGAIN

The Lake Bodom murders are among the most shocking and brutal in Finnish history. It was the summer of 1960, and four teenagers were camping at Lake Bodom near Helsinki. Sometime in the very early morning, someone or someones entered their tent, murdering three of them with a knife and a blunt object. The fourth, Nils Gustafsson, managed to survive, but sustained a concussion and a broken jaw. The police never charged anyone for the crime.

Amazingly, in 2004, more than forty years after the murders, Gustafsson was arrested and tried for the murder of his three friends. The prosecution had new evidence from an analysis of blood stains and claimed that Gustafsson had killed his new girlfriend in a jealous rage, and then killed the other two teenagers so they wouldn't turn him in. But the accusations didn't hold and Gustafsson was acquitted. The "real" murderer is still at large.

I DREAM OF SMOOTH, SILKY HAIR

Madame C. J. Walker was the first female self-made millionaire in American history. The first free child born to generations of slaves, she worked very hard from a young age as a washerwoman and laundress. In the 1890s, she developed a terrible case of dandruff and started to lose her hair. She had a dream in which "a big, black man appeared to me and told me what to mix up in my hair." She sent away for the mixture of ingredients she'd dreamt of and put it on her scalp. Within weeks, her hair was growing splendidly. She went on to found a multimillion-dollar corporation.

IT WAS A NIGHTMARE

When Stephen King had writer's block while working on his novel *It*, he had a nightmare about leeches inside of discarded refrigerators. He says he woke up and knew immediately that that was where the novel was supposed to go.

FORECAST: BUTT-KICKING

Before the Battle of Little Bighorn in 1876, Chief Sitting Bull dreamt of soldiers raining down from the sky onto his camp, and a voice saying, "I give you these because they have no ears." Sitting Bull took this dream as an omen that he would win the battle, and he did.

SINISTER SERIAL KILLERS: DELFINA AND MARIA DE JESUS GONZALEZ

Sisters Delfina and Maria were the owners of Rancho El Angel, a brothel in Guanajuato, Mexico, in the 1950s and '60s. The sisters had a successful business, but they also had a problem on their hands: the prosti-tutes who got too old to work expected continued financial support. Every good businessperson knows that carrying dead weight is unsustainable, and the sisters came up with a workable solution: killing their low-achieving sex workers. They also killed any customer who appeared to have a big wad of cash with him. When investigators finally questioned the sisters and examined their property, they found the bodies of 11 men and 80 women!

It's said that Adolf Hitler once started awake from a dream and took cover just seconds before the trench he was sleeping in was blown up by enemy fire.

EVERYTHING'S COMING UP FOOTY

In a bizarre unsolved case, eight severed feet washed up on the shores of Canada's Pacific coast over a period of approximately two years—from 2007 to 2009. Several of the feet were wearing an athletic shoe. Only one of them was identified as belonging to a man who was still alive and who was, according to the AP, "depressed." Police have attempted to match the DNA of the remaining feet to missing persons, but have yet to make any connections as of this writing.

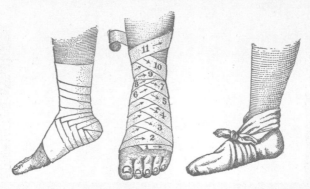

7. BAG OF TRICKS

FAMOUS MAGICIANS, HOAXES,
AND FEATS OF HUMAN ENDURANCE

And above all, watch with glittering eyes the whole world around you because the greatest secrets are always hidden in the most unlikely places. Those who don't believe in magic will never find it. —ROALD DAHL

FOR AS LONG AS THERE HAVE BEEN BELIEVERS, there have been scams. And hoaxes. Magicians of the parlor variety are known for their sleight of hand, their "bag of tricks"; but it isn't possible for the trick to work unless we, the audience, *believe*. Magicians are among the most ancient entertainers on earth—the court jester, the fool, the juggler, the advisor. In his book *Magic Words,* author Craig Conley calls magicians the earliest storytellers. Here are some of their tales—a few of the best, the worst, and some in between.

FIVE MOST DANGEROUS MAGIC TRICKS

Adapted from *DailyCognition.com: Blog of Unusual and Funny News Worldwide:*

- Underwater Straight Jacket Escape

- Frozen in Block of Ice

- Chinese Water Torture Cell

- Buried Alive

- Catching a Bullet in Your Mouth

THE CURSE OF THE BULLET CATCH

The notorious "catching a bullet in your mouth" magic trick has sent at least 15 magicians to their graves. It all started in the 1600s when a magician claiming to be capable of the feat was attacked and beaten to death by a spectator who suspected him of demonic allegiances. Two copycat magicians later killed a son and a wife by accidentally using real bullets instead of blanks, a mistake repeated by several magicians to follow. In two more cases, the stunt was sabotaged: once when an audience member put nails in the gun, and once when an angry wife loaded the gun with real bullets.

The "curse of the bullet catch" has scared many magicians into not performing the stunt. But come on, if you die while trying to catch a bullet in your mouth, can it really be said you died from a curse?

THE CURSE OF THE BULLET CATCH: PART 2

Some fates are worse than death. Consider the fate of the famous magician Chung Ling Soo, who was injured by shrapnel onstage and whisked to the hospital. There it was discovered that he was not Asian, but an American masquerading as Asian to gain exotic prestige.

TAKE A PIECE OF FRUIT!

When, in 1967, the small newspaper the *Berkeley Barb* published a satirical story claiming that smoking banana peels can get you high, nobody thought the claim would be taken seriously. But the story spread across the country, and soon the nation's wayward teenagers were "consuming" way more bananas, to the delight of clueless mothers everywhere.

The female winner of the 1980 Boston Marathon, one Rosie Ruiz, didn't exactly look like she'd just run 26 miles when she appeared at the finish line with a time of 02:31:56. That's because she hadn't. The story goes that Ruiz started the race like everyone else, then veered off course, dawdled around Boston, jumped on the subway, and rejoined the runners about a half mile from the finish line. After officials noted that she didn't appear in any of the official marathon footage or photographs from the middle part of the race, they stripped Ruiz of her title.

WITH DRAMATIC FLAIR

It was the winter of 2000, and visitors to the Swedish National Museum were having their last looks at the valuable paintings lining the walls. At the same time, three men had parked cars sideways to block both of the two roads providing access to the isolated museum and were dousing the cars with gasoline. One man lit a match, the cars went up in flames, and the heist began.

As the thieves rushed into the front entrance of the museum, they sprinkled the pavement with steel spikes sharp enough to pop car tires. One man brandished a gun. He entered the museum, shouted, "Everybody get down!" and put the gun to a museum guard's head. The other two men ran to the most valuable gallery, where a Rembrandt and two Renoirs were located. Using bolt cutters to snap the security cords that buoyed each painting, they stuffed the three masterpieces, valued at $36 million, into their bags with stunning speed. Then they bolted—all three of them—to the wharf behind the building, where an accomplice in a speedboat waited. The boat headed east to the bay, where it docked in a known fishing harbor. The men, and the million-dollar paintings, disappeared into the streets of Stockholm.

SAYS ME

In *Magic Words*, Craig Conley writes that magic phrases like "open sesame" are classically associated with opening doors. They are the keys for unlocking barriers, dissolving obstacles, revealing something beyond . . . . There is no more classic, no more straightforward magical key than open sesame."

NOT QUITE ANTS IN HIS PANTS

In 2009, an enterprising German reptile poacher was arrested in a New Zealand airport after authorities found 44 lizards sewed into pouches in his underwear. The police probably did the man a favor. Imagine sitting on a 20-hour overseas flight with lizards crawling around in your pants!

HOLY HOAXY

Not all hoaxes are carried out with mischief in mind—some are purely defensive. Crowland Abbey, established in the 9th century, was nestled into the forests of Lincolnshire, England. During the early 15th century, the neighboring Spalding Abbey claimed some of Crowland's land as its own. When the case was brought to court, the Crowland monks presented a tome called *Historia Crowlandensis* as proof of the longevity of their abbey. The volume, which consisted of land charters and historical documents, was generally accepted as real, and Crowland won the case. *Historia* was circulated widely, cited by scholars, and eventually worked into the regional history. It wasn't until the 19th century that scholars recognized it as an outright fraud. Its language was really more 14th century than 9th, and it used terms and phrasing not popular until after the book was supposedly written. It referenced universities that hadn't even existed in the 9th century and mentioned a bridge that hadn't been constructed yet.

DOGOOD AND SNODGRASS

Statesman, inventor, scientist, everyman Benjamin Franklin was, not surprisingly, a precocious youngster. He also had a dry wit, which aided him in many hijinks, the first of which he cooked up when he was 16.

In 1722, the popular *New England Courant* began printing letters by one Silence Dogood, a middle-aged widow with many opinions and a healthy dose of cynicism. In the first letter, she introduced herself and gave a brief history of her life, claiming that her father was carried away by a wave while toasting her birth. Dogood waxed poetic on all manner of things, made fun of the fashion of the time, criticized public drunkenness, and called Harvard University elitist and corrupt. The newspaper's readers loved her, and some men even wrote in with proposals of marriage. Dogood wrote 14 letters in all and then promptly disappeared. It's likely that young Franklin, the real author of the letters, tired of the prank and moved on to something more exciting, like inventing the lightning rod or bifocals.

Humorist and man of letters Mark Twain was born as Samuel Leghorn Clemens. But before he came up with Twain, he published his writings under the hilarious pseudonym Thomas Jefferson Snodgrass. Always a prankster, Twain often went to great lengths to pull off a hoax or meet his ends. Once, he convinced a San Francisco newspaper to print a story about a man who lost his fortune when he shifted his investments from mining ventures to utilities. As the story went, the man was so devastated that he spiraled into a mad, frothing rampage that ended with him murdering his entire family, running down a public street waving a bloody scalp, and finally cutting his own throat. Readers were horrified by the tale, but they were even more scandalized to learn that it was a hoax borne out of a petty feud between Twain and the utility companies.

PRESTER JOHN WHO?

Anyone who's seen a Disney movie or read about medieval unicorns knows that 12th-century Europe was a bizarre place. Cut off from contact with the East, Europeans imagined the world outside Europe as a vibrant, fairy-tale land populated with dragons, horned men, and winged beasts—not to mention gold-encrusted castles bursting at the seams with riches.

One such kingdom was believed to be that of King Prester John, a Christian from the East who was sympathetic to Europeans and eager to help them regain their military foothold on the surrounding lands. Nobody had actually seen or heard from Prester John until around 1170, when the Byzantine emperor Manuel Comnenus received a letter stamped with John's seal. The letter told of Prester John's Eastern Christian kingdom filled fantastical creatures, a fountain of eternal youth, and great wealth, and it extended Prester John's standing offer of military support to help establish Christian domination of the world. Needless to say, everyone was thrilled—even the pope, who sent his personal envoy to deliver a reply letter to Prester John. But nobody ever found John or his kingdom. And though they waited, patiently reassuring themselves that it was only a matter of time, they heard from him, ever again.

It turns out that Prester John's vanishing act wasn't the fault of an unreliable postal system. Prester John never existed, and the letter was a fake, possibly written by a Christian cleric eager to lift the Christian armies' spirits as they fought in the Crusades. But the legend of John and of fantastic Christian kingdoms of the East lived on, inspiring the voyages of thousands of hopeful explorers, treasure hunters, and missionaries for hundreds of years.

THE LYING STONES OF DR. BERINGER

Doctor, naturalist, and dean of faculty at the German University of Wurzburg, Johann Beringer was not a well-liked man. He had a reputation for being a bit of a prig, and as such, he was vulnerable to all manner of pranks and hoaxes. One day, Beringer asked some young boys to explore nearby Mount Eivelstadt and bring back any interesting rocks they found. The boys diligently returned with a box of fossils so fascinating that Beringer believed he had made a great scientific discovery. For well over a year, he asked the boys to bring him rocks from the mountain, and meanwhile, he wrote a book about his discoveries. When the book was hot off the presses, the boys approached Beringer with one final fossil: with his name carved in it. When Beringer realized that the fossils had all been fakes and that the last year of his life had been a joke, he was furious. He accused some fellow faculty members of hiring the boys to bring him fake fossils and eventually won his case. But before he did that, he frantically collected all the books he had published—an entire print run—to save himself further embarrassment.

AMEN TO THAT

In 1968, author John Macklin reported a story of Amen-Ra, an Egyptian princess who lived some 1,500 years before Christ. Macklin told the tale of the curse associated with her mummified remains. First, four young Englishmen bought her mummy, and shortly thereafter, one of them vanished into the desert, one had his arm shot off, and the other two lost all their wealth and became paupers. The next person to own the mummy suffered a fire in his home, which caused injury to three of his family members. The mummy was then given to the British Museum, whereupon the curse continued to plague all that encountered it. The delivery car that held the mummy was in an accident, one of the workers carrying the mummy fell down the stairs and broke his leg, and the other worker suffered a mysterious death.

The list goes on: A photographer who came to document the mummy committed suicide shortly thereafter. Anyone who looked at the mummy soon fell ill or even died. Reportedly, the mummy was purchased by a man who then took it on board the Titanic, and we all know how that ship's maiden voyage ended.

This amazing story was a hoax, for the mummy never existed. The British Museum has even issued an official denial. Yet the story remains in popular culture.

———◆———

Harry Houdini's birth name was Erich Weiss.

> I am sure there is magic in everything, only we have not sense enough to get hold of it and make it do things for us. —FRANCES HODGSON BURNETT, *THE SECRET GARDEN*

A GHOST OF A SCAM

In 1762, a house on Cock Lane, Smithfield, London, became known for its unusual residents: poltergeist-like apparitions. Although the events seen in the house were not unlike those of other reported hauntings, the house on Cock Lane soon became a destination as a haunted hot spot, and crowds flocked to witness the apparition. The ghost was said to be that of Mrs. Kent, the murdered wife of a former tenant. While the masses descended, many claiming to have had their own paranormal encounters, authorities investigated the current tenant of the house, a man by the name of Parsons. They suspected he had invented the spirit in order to blackmail Mr. Kent, who was still alive. After some investigation, it was revealed that the source of the disturbances was the Parson's 11-year-old daughter. Parsons was prosecuted, and his daughter was publicly pilloried.

GRAPE EXPECTATIONS

A gentleman in Louisiana gained notoriety for catching in his mouth a grape thrown from a record-setting 252 feet.

A GOOD NIGHT'S WORK

The thieves behind the 1985 pillage of Mexico's National Museum of Anthropology chose a good night to do their work. It was Christmas Eve, and the museum guards were in a celebratory mood, not paying much attention to security. It didn't help that the museum's alarm system, which had broken three years previously, hadn't been fixed yet. It wasn't until the next morning,

Christmas Day, that the morning-shift guards found that the panes had been removed from seven display cases. The thieves, who were never caught, made off with over millions of dollars worth of artifacts from the Zapotec, Maya, Aztec, and Miztec empires. One piece alone—a burial mask—would be worth up to $20 million on the black market.

FAKEOUT!

Dateline: Europe, 1944. General Dwight D. Eisenhower put his best commander—the famous General George S. Patton, veteran leader of successful military campaigns in Sicily and Italy—in charge of the First United States Army Group (FUSAG), positioned in southeast England. To the German army commanders, Patton's august presence could mean only one thing: the Allies were planning a massive attack via Pas-de-Calais, just 20 miles across the English Channel from Dover.

What the Germans didn't know is that the army under Patton's command was a complete fiction. On paper, the FUSAG comprised approximately 30 airborne, infantry, and armored divisions. On the ground, it consisted of dummy tanks, jeeps, trucks, planes, artillery, landing craft, and ships of inflatable rubber, all positioned as if poised to attack Calais. Fake military-radio traffic and dummy military bases, complete with plywood-and-canvas buildings, docks, and antiaircraft defenses, supported the ruse. Even fictitious magazine and newspaper stories, including wedding notices about fictional U.S. army personnel marrying local English girls and articles about Patton's travels in England, were published for the benefit of German intelligence. Meanwhile, Allied bombers stepped up attacks of the port of Calais, as if softening up German defenses in the area for a forthcoming invasion.

The entire deception, codenamed Operation Quicksilver, was designed to draw the Germans' attention away from the real troop buildup—which included 500 ships and 130,000 troops—preparing to invade France at Normandy on D-Day, June 6, 1944.

And it worked. Although Allied forces met stiff resistance from the German army forces stationed along the Normandy beaches, the Germans did not mobilize any additional forces to support and reinforce their defenses in the area. Instead, they held back several army divisions, including significant panzer (tank) divisions, in wait for Patton and his phantom army, who they were sure would soon come storming across the channel at Calais on the heels of the Normandy "feint."

8. IT WAS TRUE THEN

WEIRD HISTORICAL EVENTS, BELIEFS, AND PRACTICES

History is a nightmare from which I am trying to awake. —JAMES JOYCE, *ULYSSES*

OPIUM, UNICORNS, DEATH BY HANGING— history holds a treasure trove of the strange, the abhorrent, and the macabre. Mad hatter, bats, time travel . . . not all of history is doomed to repeat itself. We have in many ways learned from some of the horrors of the past, but did we lose a little delightful deviance along the way? Come now, we all like our hot water on tap and our cocktails on ice, don't we?

DING, DONG, YOU'RE WRONG!

In a historic attempt to rectify the horrors of the past, the Swiss state of Glarus exonerated Anna Goeldi of the crime of witchcraft in 2008, some two hundred years after she was beheaded for the offense. Goeldi was the last person in Europe to be executed as a witch—for such misdoings as causing another girl to spit pins and go into convulsions.

Although several thousand people, primarily women, were murdered as penalty for witchcraft, Goeldi was executed in 1782, after the now-infamous "witch craze" had passed. This made Goeldi's death especially symbolic and the public acknowledgement of innocence incredibly significant for the state of Glarus, the continent of Europe, and witches and their descendants worldwide. Both Protestant church authorities and the Roman Catholic Church were consulted in reaching the decision to absolve Goeldi and restore her good name.

THE GOOD OL' DAYS

In 1900, the tariff on perfume was 20 cents higher than the tariff on liquid opium.

HALF-HEARTED

When the poet John Keats died in Italy, his heart was removed from his body and sent back to England for burial.

BEER ME: FUN FACTS ABOUT EVERYONE'S FAVORITE LIBATION

- According to evidence found on an ancient Babylonian clay tablet, people have been brewing beer since 6000 BC.

- The first recorded beer recipe is a 4,000-year-old ode to a Sumerian beer goddess.

- The ancient Babylonians were serious about their beer. Any brewmaster who manufactured "unfit" beer was drowned in his own brew.

- Medieval Europeans believed in unicorns and dragons, and they also drank beer with breakfast. Connection? You decide.

- In the 1700s, beer was brewed extra strong so it could survive the voyage from England to colonial India.

SWING LOW

Joseph-Ignace Guillotin is credited as having intro-duced a swift and painless device designed to execute people in a humane fashion. He tested this device on the necks of corpses in the Bicêtre Hospital in Paris and, by 1789, concluded that it was significantly more rapid and effective than the common axe. Although Guillotin, after whom the guillotine is named, is wide-ly credited as having been the inventor of this device, it was, in fact, used in Italy, Germany, Scotland, and France throughout the 16th century.

A thing is not necessarily true because a man dies for it.
—OSCAR WILDE

The Dead Sea Scrolls were discovered in the Judean des-ert in 1947 when some shepherds entered a cave to find an errant goat. There they found the manuscripts, made of animal skins, papyrus, and copper, rolled up in clay jars. The shepherds never would have entered the caves if not for that mischievous goat. Talk about a lucky break!

Halloween lovers have potato blight to thank for bringing the holiday to America. Many scholars believe that Halloween has Celtic roots and that it was carried over to the States by poor Irish immigrants fleeing the great potato famine of 1841.

TRISKAIDEKAPHOBIA MANIA

Henry Ford had a severe case of triskaidekaphobia, or the fear of the number 13. He completely refused to do business on Friday the 13th.

There are countless cases of this phobia in the world today. Some blame the explosion of the Apollo 13 on its unlucky number. The Apollo 13 took off at exactly 1:13 p.m., which is 13:13 military time, on April 4, 1970, or 4/11/70—digits that add up to 13.

Franklin Delano Roosevelt would divert his plans if they fell on the thirteenth of any month. Reportedly, trains would be ordered to leave the station before midnight on the 12th or after midnight on the morning of the 14th if FDR was on board. And Roosevelt even avoided the 13th in death. He died on Thursday, April 12, 1945.

The ancient Romans and Egyptians used peach pits, which are rich in cyanide, to execute people.

A STRANGE NEW WORLD

Columbus nearly landed on the West Indies island inhabited by the Carib, an ancient tribe known for eating humans. (The word *cannibal* is derived from the Spanish word for *Carib*.) Instead, he docked on the shores of an island inhabited by a peaceful tribe known as the Arawaks.

Columbus was also the first European to bring peppers back to Europe. He "discovered" them in Hispaniola, and he liked their spicy kick, which reminded him of black pepper. According to some sources, peppers have existed basically forever; their seeds have been found in prehistoric caves.

The Germanic tribal people the Franks believed that if a person was cremated, he or she would not be able to return to the living. The ancient Greeks burned their dead soldiers to avoid desecration.

Ancient Romans used pigeon droppings to bleach their hair blonde.

PESKY FLY-AWAY HAIR?

In ancient Rome, the method for curing baldness was to smash up hundreds of houseflies and smear them onto the balding pate or thinning hair. There is no evidence that this cure actually worked, so don't try it at home. *Mummy* is the Arabic word for bitumen, which, roughly translated, means "tar." Bodies of mummies were coated with a tarlike substance.

◄———►

The ancient Greeks believed that when the body died, the soul it left in the form of a butterfly.

IT'S HARDING BEING ME

Warren G. Harding, 29th president of the United States, was a good-looking fellow, and his mix of power and handsome had women falling at his feet. When a rumor that he'd fathered a child with a woman 30 years his junior started making the rounds in Washington, D.C., Harding's wife, Florence (known as Flossie) asked the Bureau of Investigation to look into it. They confirmed that the rumor was true, and Mrs. Harding was devastated. In private, she asked an investigator about a "little white powder" that she'd heard could be discreetly mixed into a drink or food and cause death. Some months later, in August 1923, on a journey from Vancouver to San Francisco, the president became very ill and died quite suddenly. The cause was thought to be food poisoning and a heart attack, but Mrs. Harding didn't let the coroner perform an autopsy. So the world will never know whether little Florence Harding took Warren G.'s life.

NO-GO-A-GO-GO

A city ordinance dating back to 1942 declares it illegal to dance in Des Moines, Iowa, after 2 a.m.

HIDDEN MESSAGES

In 1900, the placement of a stamp on a letter had a special significance all its own. If a stamp were inverted on the right-hand upper corner, it meant the person being written to was to write no more. If the stamp were placed on the left-hand upper corner and inverted, then the writer was declaring affection for the recipient. When the stamp appeared in the top center, it signified an affirmative answer to a question, and when placed at the bottom center, a negative answer. If the stamp were on the right-hand corner at a right angle, the receiver of the letter loved the sender, but placed in the left-hand corner, the stamp indicated hatred.

LORD, WHAT FOOLS THESE MORTALS BE!

The grave of William Shakespeare, located at the Holy Trinity Church in Shakespeare's hometown of Stratford-upon-Avon, is protected by a curse the bard himself penned for his tombstone. The words, "Blest be the man that spares these stones, And curst be he that moves my bones" are inscribed on the aging headstone. But according to the local clergy, the stones above Shakespeare's grave are in an advanced state of deterioration and need to be fixed. The restoration process will be a careful one. No one wants to risk the anger of a vengeful Shakespearian ghost. We all read *Hamlet*, right?

FROM THE CRADLE TO THE GRAVE

Francis de Civille of Normandy suffered from a destiny of premature burial. According to sources as reputable as they got back in the 16th century, his mother was buried alive while still pregnant with him, and her body was exhumed so she could deliver the child. As an adult, in 1563, Civille was buried in a mass grave during his stint in the army, but his servant dug up his body and discovered he was still alive. While recovering in his own home, enemy soldiers invaded and tossed his body into a heap of manure, where he remained buried for three more days. He was once again rescued and revived. He went on to live to the ripe age of 105 and was buried three days after his death, just to be sure.

WHY IS A RAVEN LIKE A WRITING DESK?

Why was the hatter in *Alice in Wonderland* mad? For decades, hatters used mercurial solution for the felting process; the solution made fur fibers bind together and form felt. Hatters also used mercury for carrotting, a technique that colored the fibers a shade of orange. This constant exposure to high levels of mercury generally resulted in some form of mercury poisoning, and it was so widespread that the phrase "mad as a hatter" became common. Symptoms of mercurial poisoning included nerve damage, causing what was known as "the hatter's shakes." After long-term exposure, some psychological damage, including impaired judgment and sleep disorders, occurred.

However, in his 1983 article for the British Medical Journal, H. A. Waldron argued that the inspiration for Lewis Carroll's Mad Hatter was more likely a furniture dealer named Theophilus Carter. Carter, also a mathematics professor, was well known for having eccentric ideas and for always wearing a top hat. He also was an inventor, and among his more unusual inventions was an alarm clock that worked by tipping the sleeper out of bed. Waldron also argued that the psychological symptoms of mercury poisoning typically manifest as excessive timidness, shyness, anxiety, and a desire to remain unobserved and unobtrusive—traits quite unlike those of the Mad Hatter Carroll created.

SACRED SH*T

The scarab was a sacred symbol for ancient Egyptians. They likened the beetle, which rolled dung into balls and then buried them, to the god Kheper, whose job it was to roll the sun across the sky every day before burying it at night.

WHERE'S THE BEEF?

The term *Uncle Sam* dates back to the Revolutionary War and a beef inspector named Samuel Wilson, who was very popular among his employees and affectionately known as Uncle Sam. After finishing his inspection, he would send beef to a contractor named Elbert Anderson, where it was stamped *E.A.U.S.* When a worker asked what the letters stood for, a cohort replied jokingly that he didn't know, unless they stood for "Elbert Anderson and Uncle Sam." The joke spread widely. The abbreviation *U.S.* was commonly said to mean *Uncle Sam*, thus making the nickname *Uncle Sam* synonymous with *United States*.

In old Europe, it was believed that the soul of the first corpse buried in a new graveyard would belong to the devil.

Nowadays we say that a short guy who's insecure about his height has a Napoleon complex. But Napoleon wasn't that short; he was a robust five feet, six inches—average height for Frenchmen of the time. He just hung around with a lot of tall guys, making him look short in comparison.

KING CRAZYPANTS

In addition to being England's only officially insane king, King George III had a disease called porphyria, a hereditary condition that made his urine deep purple. George enjoyed nicknames like "Mad King George" and "the King Who Lost the American Colonies." He was the one who (insanely?) issued the Stamp Act that got the ball of the American Revolution rolling.

BAT BOMBERS

After the 1941 attack on Pearl Harbor, American dental surgeon Lytle S. Adams was so filled with patriotic fervor that he vowed to create a weapon to help the United States fight the Japanese. He had just been on a vacation to New Mexico, home to many species of bats, and was inspired by the hardy little flyers. Lytle drafted a proposal for equipping bats with small incendiary bombs wired with timers. The idea was to drop the bomb-toting bats at a high altitude and let them disperse about a Japanese city, where they would settle into eaves, attics, and barns to roost. Then time-delayed smoke bombs and firebombs would go off, wreaking havoc in the city.

According to palmistry, long fingers denote sensitivity, and short ones the opposite. Pointed fingertips mean imaginative ability, squared ones indicate rationality, and spatulate tips suggest an active person.

MADLY MINIATURE

In 1924, Queen Mary of England, a dollhouse connoisseur, received a 100-by-62-inch, three-story, Georgian-style miniature mansion as a gift from the people of England. The house, which took four years to furnish, was designed by famous British architect Sir Edwin Lutyens. Built upon a base packed with machinery, the miniature mansion boasted a formal garden, working hot and cold water taps, a little gramophone that played "God Save the Queen," pastry ovens fueled by tiny lumps of coal, working elevators, and a wine cellar complete with tiny bottles of real champagne.

BORN TO BE SUPERSTITIOUS

Hiding a knife under a pregnant woman's mattress is thought to cut away birth pains. Another way to guarantee an easy delivery is to unlock all the doors in the house and tie knots in the curtains.

Infamous boy pharaoh King Tut was not known for his virility and strength. Recent research has revealed that at the time of his death at age 19, Tut was suffering from a broken leg, a degenerative bone disease, and a nasty case of malaria.

Even the most dedicated Shakespearean scholar might be a bit confused by these lines in *A Midsummer Night's Dream:* "I shall desire you of more acquaintance, good Master Cobweb; if I cut my finger I shall make bold with you." But to the 17th-century Englishman, they made perfect sense: cobwebs were known to heal bleeding wounds.

The Chinese belief that pine oil promotes a long and healthy life is based on an old folk tale. Zhao Qu was gravely ill, and his family left him in the mountains to die. But before they left him, Qu was given an herbal medicine that contained pine oil. The medicine instantly revived him, and Qu found his way home and went on to live 100 healthy, vibrant years.

Have you ever wondered how the characters in Jane Austen novels spread gossip so fast? Between the late

1700s and the early 1800s, in a time before email and cell phones, teenage girls depended on snail mail to spread news far and wide. The British postal service cooperated, delivering mail up to six times a day.

I'VE GOT TO HAND IT TO YOU

In early 20th-century Europe, it was believed that the hand of a dead person, especially that of a man who had been executed for murder or another crime, was imbued with healing agents. One woman claimed to have been cured of a strawberry birthmark with the touch of a dead man's hand, and it was also said to cure lumps, swellings, and other skin problems.

The 1949 drought that caused New York City officials to curb use of lawn sprinklers and swimming pools also prompted Roman Catholics to issue special prayers for rain. The prayers weren't called off until the following December.

The ancient Greeks were probably the first civilization to keep houseplants. About 2,500 years ago, they kept exotic plants from India and Persia in small terrariums around the house. Because horticulture was traditionally a maid or servant's work, the wealthy found cultivating indoor plants to be a novel and exciting practice.

HIS HEART WASN'T IN IT

One of the creepiest statues ever sculpted is Ligier Richier's 1547 depiction of the rotting corpse of Prince René de Chalon in a Bar-le-Duc, France, church. According to legend, the prince, who died at age 25, requested that his likeness be "not a standard figure but a life-size skeleton with strips of dried skin flapping over a hollow carcass, whose right hand clutches at the empty rib cage while the left hand holds high his heart in a grand gesture." The prince got what he asked for—the sculpture is positively garish, portraying a half-decomposed skeleton man with his empty hand held high. The shriveled heart, which once made its home in hand, was supposedly stolen sometime around the French Revolution.

The most highly regarded thieves of the 19th century were the safecrackers—men who tested their mettle by cracking every new safe on the market, with the help of drills, explosives, and even artillery. One of these men was minister-turned-thief Herbert Wilson, who worked as an apprentice in a safe factory, studied welding, and assembled a crack safe-robbing team. Wilson amassed $15 million from targets as big as Sinclair Oil before he was arrested and served 20 years behind bars.

A STRANGE PATERNITY TEST

In some primitive societies, it was believed that a father endured as much birthing pain as a mother. Therefore, to discover the paternity of a baby born out of wedlock, all a village had to do was see which man groaned in pain when the mother started giving birth.

TALES FROM SOME CRYPTS

Incorruptibility is the belief held by some Christians and Eastern Orthodox religions that supernatural forces prevent the bodies of the particularly pious from decomposing. These special someones are said to emit the Odour of Sanctity, a sweet, pleasant smell, after dying. One example of incorruptibility is the naturally preserved body of Zita, patron saint of Lucca, who has been on full display in an Italian church since 1580. A devoted and pious peasant girl who worked as a housekeeper, Zita was rewarded for her generosity and devotion with a series of miracles over the course of her life. When she died in 1272, her fame spread, and she was even mentioned in Dante's *Inferno*. Her wizened body was exhumed in 1580, found to be incorruptible, and placed in a silver casket in her local church. Zita was canonized as the patron saint of Lucca in 1696.

In 1994, workers restoring an old church in Vác, Hungary, uncovered a 200-year-old crypt holding 265 coffins, each hand-painted and stacked according to size. For reasons that scientists cannot quite pinpoint, the coffins and the bodies inside them had been perfectly preserved, down to the clothing, rosaries, and trinkets enclosed in each. The preserved bodies also provided a clue about their cause of death: small traces of tuberculosis.

The crypt beneath the Capuchin Church in Brno in the Czech Republic contains the perfectly preserved bodies of 24 monks, who, out of piety and poverty, used the same coffin over and over again. After funerary rites, the dead body was removed from the coffin and placed carefully on a bed of bricks in the cool, airy crypt. A combination of topsoil and dry air currents apparently kept the bodies from decomposing, and they are on display to this day, their mostly peaceful expressions permanently etched in their rubbery faces.

I SAID, JUST A TRIM PLEASE!

In medieval times, barbers doubled as surgeons, especially on the battlefield—until the surgeons broke off from the barbers in 1745. Now the only link that remains betweens barbers and their surgical past is the red-and-white-striped barber's pole, representing a long bandage around the arm of a surgical patient. Bloodletting was also once on a barber's list of duties.

AMERICAN FOLK SAYINGS

"A wife who does not know how to keep house throws out more with a teaspoon than a man brings in with a shovel."

"A man is the only animal that can be skinned more than once."

"Be silent and pass for a philosopher."

"Even a fish wouldn't get caught if he kept his mouth shut."

TURKISH FOLK SAYINGS

"An ass does not appreciate fruit compote."

"Do not search for a calf under an ox."

NOT SO RAWSOME

In medieval times, eating raw vegetables was considered unhealthy. Medieval diners would consider subscribers to the trendy raw-food diet completely insane.

EELS: NOT JUST FOR SUSHI ANYMORE

This cure for warts dates back to 1250:

One procures a live eel, fresh or salt water species are both acceptable, and cuts its head off. Then one anoints those parts of the body afflicted with warts, using the hot blood of the eel. Allow to stand until the blood dries and do not wash the body parts so treated for at least three days.

Bury the head of the eel deeply within the earth. Remember where you buried it, so you can check its decomposition—if required.

As the head of the eel rots over time, the warts will disappear. This cure generally works better in the summer months, because the eel's head rots faster.

CHRISTMAS SURPRISE

One blustery Christmas evening in 1926, patients started stumbling into the emergency room at Bellevue Hospital in New York City. One man was experiencing serious hallucinations and believed he was being chased by a deranged Santa Claus with a knife. Others were just terribly ill, doubled over in agonizing pain. By the end of that day, doctors counted more than 60 visits from people who believed they had simply "had too much to drink." At that time, alcohol was outlawed by the Volstead Act (formerly the Prohibition Act), and people had to procure their, ahem, spirits, from unseemly sources. Much of the alcohol available on the black market was moonshine or "bathtub gin," filled with harmful chemicals and metals, and it frequently made people sick. But the people who showed up at the emergency room that Christmas had ingested even more dangerous substances—small amounts of methyl alcohol, put in the liquor courtesy of the U.S. government. It seems that the government was deliberately poisoning the raw materials used to alcohol, supposedly in an effort to discourage bootleggers from distributing illegal libations.

CATS: NOT OUTSIDE THE LAW

Dogs and cats didn't always enjoy the privileged status they do today. In medieval times, they could be tried and condemned for crimes, just like humans. In the late 1730s, a group of printer's apprentices in Paris felt they were being done an injustice by the master's wife's cats, who were constantly begging for scraps and screeching at night. A trial was staged, complete with guards, a confessor, and a public executioner. The unfortunate cats were pronounced guilty and strung up on cat-sized gallows. When the master and his wife got home, the apprentices were laughing hysterically, delirious with happiness. Justice had been served!

THE NOSE KNOWS

Face reading is a form of fortune-telling popular in China. Your eyebrows represent your state of mind; your eyes, your worldview; and your nose, your approach to all things financial. If the tip of your nose points right, you probably spend more money on other people than on yourself. If it points left, the opposite is true. If it is centered, you spend money in a balanced manner.

One of the popular exhibits at the Egyptian Museum in Cairo is the "screaming mummy," so named for the painful expression on his face. For many years experts have speculated about just how this man, who is widely believed to have been a prince, perished. One theory is that he was buried alive, and his agonized, dropped-jaw facial expression reflects the last moments he gulped for precious air.

BACK FROM THE FUTURE

In 2001, visitors to several online bulletin boards began to take notice of an anonymous poster's bizarre claims and wacky stories. The poster purported to be a soldier from the future—2036 to be exact—who was visiting 2001 under military orders to bring back an IBM 5100 computer. Eventually the poster offered up a name, John Titor, and some compelling information about the future. He said that by 2015, the United States would be ravaged by a massive nuclear war and eventually split into five different regions, each with its own president. Thousands of lives would be lost to a rare brain disorder linked to mad cow disease. Titor's grasp of time-travel theory was so solid that some people believed that he was truly a visitor from the future. But others thought his ideas about time travel were based too heavily on present knowledge; if he was truly from 2036, he'd be thinking on a whole different wavelength.

World, do not ask those snatched from death where they are going, they are always going to their graves.
—NELLY SACHS

CHAPTER EIGHT: IT WAS TRUE THEN   171

A DELIGHTFUL TRADITION

Every Christmas, residents of the small Swedish village of Gavle turn out to vandalize an effigy of a goat they call Yule Goat. The crafting of straw goats has long been a Nordic seasonal tradition, but Gavle took it several steps further when, in 1966, a public-relations consultant had the idea of building a giant goat in the town center to draw publicity. That first year, the enormous Yule Goat caught fire at the stroke of midnight. Subsequent Yule Goats have suffered car crashes, piece-by-piece destruction, and burnings. It turns out that residents of Gavle, quiet as they are, have a shared interest in wrecking things.

9. TALES FROM THE CRYPTIDS

MYTHOLOGICAL BEINGS, FREAKY CREATURES, AND CRYPTOZOOLOGICAL SIGHTINGS

Facts are fine, fer as they go . . . but they're like water
bugs skittering atop the water. Legends, now—
they go deep down and bring up the heart of a story.
—MARGUERITE HENRY, *MISTY OF CHINCOTEAGUE*

I HAD TO RESERVE A CHAPTER FOR A SMATTERING
of the kind of stories that are a *different* kind of strange—
and possibly only legend. While I would like to think
that the majority of what I research is quite true (this
making it even more bizarre!), I do encounter stories
and myths of fantastic quality. Since I believe that most
fiction is rooted in truth, I am sure that the *chupacabra*
and the *sasquatch* of legend must have some merit. And
they certainly play a valuable role in our society—how
else would we explain, late at night around the dying
embers of a campfire, that unearthly glow emanating
just beyond the circle?

The term *cryptozoology*—the science of hidden animals—was invented in the 1950s by Bernard Heuvelmans.

A bunyip is an aboriginal Australian monster that is known for jumping out of watering holes and scaring passersby. He is huge, hairy, and loud.

MEET CHESSIE

The American version of Scotland's Loch Ness monster is Chessie, a monster that makes her home on Chesapeake Bay, near the nation's capital. Reported sightings of Chessie describe her as 30 to 40 feet long and snake-like, with a football-shaped head. One Chessie sighting took place in the summer of 1984, when a fisherman idly observed some bluefin jumping clear of the water as he floated past Caddy Corner. All of a sudden, all bluefin activity stopped, and the ocean was eerily quiet for a moment as Chessie soundlessly glided past.

To release a zombie from its bondage, give it salted water or salted food, and it will drag itself back to its grave.

Lobsters have blue blood.

THE JERSEY DEVIL

There are several versions of the origins of the Jersey Devil, but the most common says that in 1735, Mother Leeds, frustrated to find herself pregnant with her 13th child, wished the child to be a devil. Her wish was granted. Shortly after the child was born, it fled to the woods, and the legend of the Jersey Devil was born. In January 1909, both New Jersey and Pennsylvania were reportedly terrorized by a devil-like creature. More than 1,000 witnesses provided eerily similar descriptions of the beast they had seen. Hunters organized a posse, but to no avail. Sightings of the devil continued well into the 1960s, but at the time of this writing no recent sightings had been widely reported.

A Spectre has first choice, by right,
In filling up a vacancy;
Then Phantom, Goblin, Elf, and Sprite—
If all these fail them, they invite
The nicest Ghoul that they can see.
—LEWIS CARROLL, FROM "PHANTASMAGORIA," CANTO I

BIGFOOT?

According to an account reported to *Phantoms and Monsters*, in November 2007, a Michigan woman and her husband were home one evening watching TV when they heard two gunshots coming from next door. The husband quickly got dressed and headed to his neighbor's house, where he expected that the neighbor, Bob, was warding off the bear that had been sighted in the area lately.

Bob had let his two dogs outside before bed, as he did every night. One of the dogs took its usual romp toward the woods, but stopped suddenly and then cowered. When Bob saw this, he assumed the dog had seen a bear, so he headed outside with his rifle. That is when he looked up to see a dark figure, standing upright at about six feet, seven inches tall. Thinking it was a human, he shouted at it. The creature looked at Bob and then walked back into the woods, this time on all fours. The most unusual thing, Bob said later, was the creature's eyes—they glowed red.

Bob aimed his shotgun at the beast's chest, which is when he noticed it had no fur. He fired and hit it, but the creature did not move. The figure stood upright again, and Bob fired again, but this time he missed. The figure disappeared into the woods. No blood or tracks were discernable.

In 1903 an inventor was refused a patent for his unique invention: a pair of eyeglasses for chickens who may be exposed to the aggressive eye pecking of other pullets.

We must not look at goblin men,
We must not buy their fruits:
Who knows upon what soil they fed
Their hungry thirsty roots?
—CHRISTINA ROSSETTI, "GOBLIN MARKET"

HIP-HOP HORROR

In April 1973 a giant kangaroolike creature was encountered in Enfield, Illinois, by the McDaniel family. The children heard something scratching at the door, trying to get into the house. Later that evening, Mr. McDaniel heard the beast return and went to the door to greet it with a pistol. What he saw shocked him to his core: a five-foot-tall being, grayish in color, with a short trunk, three legs, two short arms, and huge pink eyes.

Recovering from his initial shock, McDaniel shot at the creature several times, but it bounded away, hissing. When state troopers arrived, they found tracks that looked doglike, except for the distinguishing characteristic of six toe pads.

But the story doesn't end there. Several days later, Mr. McDaniel was awakened by dogs howling. When he went to investigate, he discovered the creature walking along the railroad tracks near his home.

Since then, there have been numerous sightings of the creature by locals, and similar sightings have been reported in the Chicago area as well.

AT LEAST THEY'RE COURTEOUS

In *The Weiser Field Guide to Cryptozoology*, Deena West Budd warns:

> If you are ever walking by the river after dark and encounter a group of children playing in the moonlight, you might want to take a closer look. They might not be children at all, and they probably are not playing! You might be seeing a group of kappa, amphibious cryptids often mistaken for six- and seven-year-old children. Kappa are fishy, eat children and cucumbers, and are said to be very polite.

THE LITTLE THINGS THAT COUNT

Ever heard of a clurichaun? This tiny relative to the Irish leprechaun is so fond of wine that he protects wine cellars and casks. Perhaps this is the reason that clurichauns are spotted in parts of Italy and known as *monicellos*. You can invite one to your home by leaving a little wine out before you go to bed. Just be warned before you do it: you must be sure that you have an ample supply of wine for him to drink. Otherwise, he will cause what little wine you may have to spoil and will wreak havoc in general.

WELL, I GUESS I'M A GHOUL THEN

What's a ghoul, you ask? According to *Dictionary.com,* a ghoul is "an evil spirit or demon in Muslim folklore believed to plunder graves and feed on corpses; one who delights in the revolting, morbid, or loathsome."

WEREWOLVES IN GERMANY

On October 31, 1589, a man named Peter Stubb was put to death in Cologne, along with his daughter and mistress. Their crime? Werewolfism. Stubb was accused of terrorizing the German city for 25 years after accepting a magic belt from Satan that would turn him into a werewolf. Stubb's body was broken on a huge wheel, and then he was decapitated and burnt with his "co-conspirators." The authorities never found the magic belt—Satan had apparently snatched it back just in time.

BONNY GOOSE EGGS?!

An item of special curiosity appeared in the 1824 *Scottish Gallovidian Encyclopedia*. A short entry, wedged between some notes on linguistics, noted a fellow named Jock Mulldroch, who lived 150 years ago, saying, "Tradition has it that he laid eggs, ay eggs, larger than goose eggs, and strangely speckled black and yellow; he used to cackle too after he laid them." Mulldroch laid an egg once a fortnight; his mother sold some as "bonny goose eggs," but she placed two others under a hen and waited for them to hatch. When they did, out from the thick shells popped two little men dressed in green. (How did they get clothes in there?) The townspeople called these two jolly fellows Willie and Wattie Birly, and they lived happily until a great snowstorm buried them.

CHILDREN EATEN WHILE U WAIT

France had a huge werewolf problem in the 16th century. You couldn't even get your pants hemmed without putting up with a little lycanthropy. The tailor of Chalons was sentenced to death for luring children into his shop and tearing them to pieces with his teeth, then eating them like a wolf. Police discovered a cask of bones in his house, and the details of the subsequent trial were apparently so grotesque the judge had the documents burned.

MEDIEVAL CHILDREN

Think kids these days are bad? In 1598, a young peasant girl named Pernette Gandillon roved like a wild animal around the Jura Mountains, between France and Switzerland. One day, she came upon a little boy and girl picking strawberries, and she pounced on the girl, intent to kill. When the little boy defended his sister with a pocket knife, Gandillon wrestled the knife from his hand and slashed his throat. He was four years old. The people of the village were so horrified by the event they tore Gandillon to pieces. Oh yeah, she was also a werewolf.

I KNOW YOU'RE OUT THERE . . .

The crested bellbird of the Australian and Venezuelan wetlands distracts its predators by throwing its voice from tree to tree, like a ventriloquist.

NOT A PRETTY SIGHT

When a walrus is feeling warm, its skin turns pink.

THIRD EYE'S THE CHARM

The tuatara's third eye, located squarely on the top of its head, may be used as a light sensor to help the reptile keep track of how long it's been in the sun. It may also work as a kind of lizard GPS, using the sun's position in the sky to guide the tuatara towards home.

The world's smallest vertebrate is the *Paedocypris progenetica*, a tiny type of carp that grows up to 1 cm (0.4 inches) long.

ARACHNOPHOBIA x A MILLION

A terrifying new species of spider has been discovered skittering along the Jordan-Israel border. It's got a positively scary set of specs: it has a 5.5-inch (14-cm) legspan, is nocturnal, and is most active during the summer heat. It's also a proponent of the sit-and-wait hunting technique, which means it waits around, biding its time and energy, until you innocently happen upon its horrifying black-and-white body, and then it . . . well, it probably spiders away. But it's still scary as hell to see.

A GIANT LIE

A strange rumor had 1766 London all abuzz. Commodore John Byron had just returned from a long sea journey, and he and his crewmembers were said to have encountered a strange tribe of 12-foot giants in Patagonia, South America. This claim didn't come out of nowhere—it was commonly believed that fantastic creatures lived beyond the threshold of exploration of the time. The story eventually appeared in print all over the place. It was a full seven years before Byron was willing to speak on the rumor. He admitted that he and his crew *had* seen a tribe of giants, but that the tallest "giant" was just six feet, six inches tall, not twelve feet.

The only food that is blue is the blueberry, and the only animal that's all purple is the South African blesbok, a breed of antelope. The animal is actually just really bright brown, but its coat has a sheen that makes it appear purple.

MONGOLIAN DEATH WORM

Squirming around somewhere beneath the Gobi desert is the Mongolian Death Worm, a truly gruesome creature named for its resemblance to a blood-filled intestine. It has spiked protrusions on its head and tail, but because it has no eyes or discernable mouth, it's hard to tell which end is which. The worm was first described in a 1926 book by Professor Roy Chapman Andrews, a paleontologist.

FROGMEN OF LOVELAND

Cryptid skeptics believe that there isn't enough evidence to prove that certain cryptids actually exist. Without photographs, video, or audio, how can we truly know that something is real? Corroborating accounts, that's how. The frogmen of Loveland are an example of a type of cryptid captured only *in* people's shared experiences. In May 1955, one man traveling through Loveland, Ohio, at 3:30 a.m. reported seeing three humanoid creatures standing by the side of the road. They had some human features, but were decidedly reptilian, with "leathery skin" and "webbed hands and feet." Months later, a woman swimming in an Ohio river was pulled under by an unidentified creature. She emerged covered in scratches and with a greenish handprint on her leg. Then, a decade later, a policeman saw a frogman, and then another officer saw another one. The frogmen are said to be completely harmless, but I would avoid a kiss from one if I were given the opportunity.

MISFORTUNE IN HER FACE

In the winter of 1814, London was atwitter with rumors of a pig-faced lady living in high style somewhere in the city. The woman was said to be enormously wealthy and the daughter of a nobleman, but she was completely closed off from society. Several Londoners wrote in to a newspaper claiming to have seen her, veiled and covered up, inside a carriage. The newspapers enthusiastically promoted the rumor, printing marriage proposals and offers of companionship in their advertisements sections. One of them, from the *Morning Chronicle*, went like this:

> *Secrecy. A single Gentleman, aged thirty-one, of a respectable Family, and in whom the utmost Confidence may be reposed, is desirous of explaining his Mind to the Friends of a Person who has a Misfortune in her Face, but is prevented for want of an Introduction . . . (1815).*

After a while, the editors of the Times and other newspapers grew tired of the rumor and pointed out that the same story had been fashionable in London 50 years prior, in 1764, at which time a man wrote in offering to make "her Sowship" an ivory trough to feed from.

THE WAY OF THE DODO

Now extinct, the dodo was a flightless bird native to the Indian Ocean island of Mauritius. The typical dodo was lumpy, fat, and rather clumsy. It had a roundly hooked beak and big bug eyes. Though there is much debate about the cause of the dodo's extinction, it is generally accepted that the bird's fearlessness, due to the lack of predators on the isolated island, and its flightlessness contributed to its demise.

10. NATURALLY STRANGE

INTERESTING INSECTS, BIZARRE PLANTS, AND ANIMAL ODDITIES

Nothing, perhaps, is strange, once you have accepted life itself, the great strange business which includes all lesser strangeness.

—ROSE MACAULAY, *CREWE TRAIN*

CORPSE FLOWERS. BLOODSUCKING GNATS. Screaming caterpillars. The natural world is sometimes more Edward Gorey than Charles Darwin, especially when you look under rocks, beneath rotting stumps, and under your nails. This chapter got started the day I bought an *Amoraphallus* for my garden and morphed (pun intended) into a collection of some of the oddest anomalies from nature. A boundless topic, I quickly had to curb my passions—I could write a whole book just about the perfectly and naturally strange.

SIREN SONG

Some believe today that the infamous mermaids spotted by sailors of yore were actually manatees. Manatees can grow to be more than 1,000 lbs.

Thirty-two of the 42 known species of bats in the United States live in Texas.

Who knows
How many crows
Goes
In a Murder of Crows?
—JAN DRANTRELL

LITTLE MISS MUFFET WOULD FAINT

In October 2008, the *Daily Telegraph* U.K. ran a story about a spider eating a bird that had been caught in its web—a bird more than twice the size of the rather large spider. In a backyard just outside of Cairns, Australia, the chestnut-breasted manikin had flown into the web of a golden orb weaver and became trapped in the thick, silky fibers. Orb weavers are known for their particularly intricate and strong webs, some of which are known to hold more than a pound of weight. Accompanying the article and soon circulating on the Internet was the picture of the golden orb weaver spider munching away on the bird. While golden orb spiders are known to prey on large insects, experts doubted that the spider would be able to consume the entire bird.

TINY AND POWERFUL

The grain amaranth was first cultivated more than 5,000 years ago in Mexico. The amaranth was considered a sacred, life-giving plant and was often used in ceremonial offerings.

Amaranth seeds were used to make flour. One amaranth seed is not quite one millimeter in diameter.

Amaranth crop production almost completely ended after the Spanish conquest of Mexico, because the conquistadores thought the rituals surrounding the sacred plant were horrific. They destroyed amaranth crops and temples where amaranth ceremonies took place, and they forbade the growing of amaranth. Gardeners who grew it were subject to punishment, including having their hands chopped off.

HONEYED MYTH

When scavenging bee hives, bears are not, in fact, in search of the honey. They do eat the honey, but that is not their primary goal. Bears actually eat bees, their pupae, and their larvae.

Crazy people who are judged to be harmless are allowed an enormous amount of freedom ordinary people are denied. —KATHERINE PETERSON, *JACOB HAVE I LOVED*

Azaleas and rhododendrons contain *andromedotoxin,* a toxin that can cause nausea, paralysis, and even death.

More than 2,000 plant species contain cyanide.

Eggplants contain solanine, a bitter toxin, as well as high levels of nicotine and histamine.

DIGESTING DIONAEA

The Venus flytrap *(Dionaea muscipula)* is one of group of carnivorous plants that attract, kill, digest, and absorb small insects. Native to boggy areas where soils lack key nutrients, this unique plant has adapted a way to absorb nutrients in addition to those it gets from photosynthesis. The flytrap lures flies, gnats, and small insects to itself by producing sweet nectar. When the insects land on a leaf to feed, the flytrap's two leaves snap closed. The more the insect struggles, the more it triggers tiny hairs that act as a mechanism to create an even tighter enclosure. The insect generally dies of a lack of air, but may also die from the digestive secretions the plant immediately begins to produce. Essentially, the insect becomes slowly liquefied and is then absorbed back into the cell walls of the plant.

In a similar fashion, the pitcher plant (*Nepenthes* sp. and *Sarracenia* sp.) and the cobra lily (*Darlingtonia californica*) attract insects by producing a glorious nectar. This nectar is usually found just inside the plants' tubular openings. Once inside, the interior of the "tube," or "pitcher," is covered in tiny, downward-facing hairs. The insect struggles to free itself, but the hairs act as a slide. Eventually, the insect ends up drowning in the small reservoir of water at the base of the tube, and the plant begins to secrete an enzyme to digest its prey.

There are several other species of carnivorous plants, including the *Cephalotus* sp. and *Heliamphous* sp.

In addition, some forms of bromeliads are suspected to be carnivorous.

Smokey the Bear, that icon of forest-fire safety, was originally named Hotfoot Teddy.

A polar bear's liver contains enough vitamin A to poison a human being.

BEYOND THE VEIL

Scientists at the University of California, Berkeley, led by Xiang Zhang, announced in August 2008 that they developed a way to cloak three-dimensional objects using artificial materials to redirect light around the objects, essentially creating a cloak of invisibility. Harry Potter fans are sure to line up early for the first commercial version of this invisibility cloak!

AND IN THIS CORNER . . .

The bumble bee bat of Thailand is the world's smallest bat, weighing about the same as a single penny. The giant flying fox of Indonesia is the world's biggest bat, with a wingspan of 6 feet (1.8 m)!

Malyasian fruit bats lactate.

Bats hang upside down because of weak legs. They would topple over if they tried to stand.

> No object is mysterious. The mystery is your eye.
> —ELIZABETH BOWEN, *THE HOUSE IN PARIS*

HOT DOC

In the *Oxford Book of the Occult,* Brian Inglis includes the story of a Pennsylvania man who appeared to have spontaneously combusted. In 1966, an employee of the local gas company, while performing his meter-reading rounds in Coudersport, Pennsylvania, entered the house of a retired doctor. The gas man discovered a pile of ash with what looked like blue smoke hanging over it. His search for the doctor uncovered some curious remains: the doctor's foot, still in its shoe. When the county coroner arrived, he discovered that the ash was, in fact, the remains of the doctor and that there was a small hole in the floor beneath the shoe. The ash had dropped through the hole onto the floor below, where the gas man had discovered it. The gas man did not report a smell like that of burning flesh, but rather the smell of what he called a new central-heating system at work. The doctor's robe, which was in the bathroom, was barely singed, and there were minimal signs of fire in the bathroom—a blackened floor, but no bubbled or blistered paint. Had the good doctor spontaneously combusted?

Humans remain fertile about the same amount of time as chimpanzees, although the human life span is longer.

Nature goes her own way, and all that to us seems an exception is really according to order. —JOHANN WOLFGANG GOETHE

THE SCREAMING CATERPILLAR

In 1990, Dr. Phillip J. DeVries published a study in which he identified not only caterpillars that screamed, but also the nature of their screams and the reason behind them. The caterpillars have two sets of organs—one behind the head, shaped like grooved rods, and one that protrudes from the top of the head—that, when rubbed together, produce a sound DeVries described as being like that of a comb running over the edge of a table. The "screams" are actually a call to arms for troops of ants, who come to protect the caterpillars from predatory wasps. The caterpillars secrete amino acids as a reward for the ants.

HOT DUCK

Each year the U.S. Fish and Wildlife Service requires hunters to purchase a duck stamp. The proceeds of the sale go to the National Wildlife Refuge System, to preserve waterfowl habitat. But 2008 left some hunters with a wet taste in their mouth. Anyone wishing to purchase the 2008 northern pintail duck stamps over the phone were greeted not by the voice of an efficient government agent, but rather by the sultry tauntings of a phone-sex line. A printing error advertising a number to call to order the stamps was one digit off, leading callers to 1-800-TRAMP24 instead of 1-800-STAMP24. The cost of reprinting was so extensive that the agency decided not to correct the mailing. Perhaps unsurprisingly, the agency received no complaints about the mistake.

> Mystery creates wonder, and wonder is the basis of man's desire to understand. —NEIL ARMSTRONG

SPINNING GOLD

The golden orb spider of Madagascar can grow to the size of a small adult human hand and produces an incredibly strong silk. The silk is so strong that Simon Peers, a British art historian, and Nicholas Godley, an American fashion designer, along with more than a million spiders and a team of spider handlers, harvested the silk and created an 11-foot-long (3.35 m), golden-hued piece of cloth. Made entirely of the silk from the golden orb spider, it is the first recorded textile of its kind.

WHEN ANIMALS ATTACK

When teased or attacked by a predator, the Spanish ribbed newt has a unique system of defense. It pushes out its ribs until they pierce its skin, exposing the ends of the bones. These bones secrete a poison, and pricking one of these barbs is fatal for the predator. The newts suffer no known ill effects from this amazing defense mechanism.

ITCHY AND SCRATCHY SHOW

Nearly 100 cats were killed in a fire at an animal shelter in Oshawa, Canada, in December 2008. Investigators believe the blaze was caused by mice or rats chewing through electrical wires in the ceiling.

The stinkhorn fungus looks delicate, but smells like rotting flesh.

A leech can consume 10 times its weight.

PIG IN BOOTS

As a piglet only six weeks old, Cinders suffered from mysophobia—a fear of dirt. Unable to coax the little piggy into the mud, where all the other piglets played, English farm owners Andrew and Debbie Keeble were at a loss until their 12-year-old daughter, Ellie, offered an ingenious solution. She suggested putting tiny Wellington boots on Cinders. Once shod in his new Wellies, lo and behold, Cinders delicately walked into the mud.

A polar bear can stay underwater for about two minutes and can swim up to 6 mph.

WILDLIFE WILDFIRE

In October 2008, a wildfire broke out near the town of Redding, California. The cause of the ferocious blaze? A flaming squirrel. Apparently, a squirrel shorted out a power line and fell to the dry vegetation below, sparking the fire.

The Dutchman's Pipe or pipevine is one of nature's stranger vines. The flowers of the variety native to the deserts of Sonora, *Aristolochia watsonii*, are pollinated by bloodsucking gnats that mistake the fleshy red bloom for a rodent's ear.

OUTHOUSE OBSERVATIONS

The mountain tree shrew (*Tupaia Montana*) of Borneo has been observed using the pitcher plant's distinctive "pitcher" as a toilet! Scientists from the University of Cambridge used a video camera to observe the shrew jumping onto the plant, licking the nectar from the underside of the leaf, and then defecating into the pitcher-like tubes. The plants secrete an enzyme that breaks down small insects, and apparently also the waste of the tree shrew!

LITTLE ZOMBIES

In Texas, the fire ant, one of the South's biggest pests, is facing a new predator of its own. Researchers at Texas A&M University have introduced a tiny phorid fly, originally native to South America, to lay their eggs onto fire ants. These eggs hatch into maggots inside the ant and begin to eat away at the ants' brains, essentially turning the fire ants into tiny little zombies. The ants wander around for up to two weeks while the maggots eat away at their brains, until the ants' heads fall off. Then the maggot turns into a fly and is ready to start the cycle over again.

Researchers expect the phorid fly to put a dent in the fire-ant population. Let's just hope the flies don't decide to try on human brains for size.

I would like to see anyone, prophet, king or God, convince a thousand cats to do the same thing at the same time.
—NEIL GAIMAN

⤙ *Myomancy* is divination by rats or mice.

⤙ *Lithomancy* is divination by stones.

⤙ *Ooscopy* and *oomantia* are methods of using eggs for divination.

⤙ *Ornithomancy* is a method of divining the future through the flight or song of birds.

⤙ *Pyromancy* is divination by fire.

⤙ The practice of telling the future by atmospheric phenomena is known as *aeromancy*.

⤙ *Aleuromancy* is divination with flour, *alomancy* is divination with salt, and *alphitomancy* is divination via barley meal or barley bread.

KINETIC CHLOROPHYLL

Cleve Backster ran an interrogation school for the New York police officers, but he gained fame from his experiments with plants and psychokinesis. Backster attached his polygraph, which he was in charge of instructing students how to use, to a potted plant. When the plant was thoroughly watered, the poloygraph recorded a reaction that, in humans, would be read as pleasure. Intrigued, Backster continued his experiments by attempting to scald the plant with hot coffee, which caused no reaction. He then thought about burning the plant, and just the thought caused the polygraph pen to jump. Next, he had a student come into a room with two plants. The student destroyed one of the plants, and then the second plant was hooked up to the polygraph machine. A series of students paraded in front of the plant, but only the one who had killed the first plant elicited a response. Backster continued to experiment, and his findings were published in the 1968 edition of *The International Journal of Parapsychology*.

The coastal taipan of Australia is one of the world's most deadly snakes. It injects the most venom per bite:

about 120 mg. Just 1 mg is enough to kill a human.

The *Mirabillis Liber* is a collection of predictions regarding saints and sibyls and is attributed to Saint Césaire (470–543 CE). The 1522 edition correctly prophesied the French Revolution.

IF YOU LIKE 'EM LEGGY

The goliath bird-eating spider, which calls South American rainforests home, has *legs* that grow up to 10 inches (25.4 cm) long. The smallest spider lives in western Samoa; the *Patu marplesi* is only 0.018 inches (0.045 cm) long.

The larvae of the jewel beetle can live 30 years or more before becoming adult insects.

The North American whippoorwill is the only bird that hibernates.

Grebes eat their own feathers.

Bracken Cave in Texas hosts the world's largest bat colony, comprising about 20 million bats.

At just 2.2 inches (5.6 cm) long and 0.056 oz. (1.6 g), the bee hummingbird is the world's smallest bird.

Scorpions can go for a year without eating and can live for up to 15 years.

GREAT BALLS OF FIRE

Ball lightning is a strange natural phenomenon that has baffled scientists for decades. Occurring after a lightning storm, it consists of bright lights, about the size of footballs, that hover over the ground and are able to pass through walls and large objects. In 1970, the Australian wife of a physicist observed ball lightning inside her bedroom. Another eyewitness saw what looked like ball lightning inside an airplane, traveling slowly down the passenger aisle. One possible explanation for ball lightning is that when lightning strikes a surface containing silica and carbon, the heat transforms these chemicals into carbon dioxide and nanoparticles of silicon, which form a ball shape. They shimmer and glow as the silicon oxidizes.

THAT'S SOME STUMP!

Perhaps the most interesting feature of Oregon's Crater Lake is a tree stump, about 9 meters (29.5 feet) in diameter, that has been bobbing vertically in the lake's waters for over a century. The earliest observations of the stump, which is known colloquially as the Old Man of the Lake, were made by geologist Joseph Diller in 1896. By tying a length of wire around the tree, Diller was able to establish that the stump was mobile; indeed, in 1938, it was observed moving more than 62 miles around Crater Lake, all the while remaining in its vertical position.

GLOW, WORM, GLOW!

In New South Wales, Australia, an army of glowworms uses the Newnes railroad tunnel, closed up in 1932, as its base of operations. The glowworms, which are actually a form of gnat that hunts with glowing threads of mucus, apparently commandeered the tunnel because it's dark and cool, providing perfect glowing conditions for the little guys.

SERIAL KILLER OF THE WASP WORLD

The appropriately named solitary wasp lives alone, building its tube-shaped nest all by itself. While its larvae are gestating, the wasp sneaks around its neighborhood, paralyzing smaller insects with its stinger and bringing them to its nest en masse. When the eggs hatch, the small, wingless wasps have plenty of fresh prey to feed on.

A TONGUE FOR A TONGUE

The *Cymothoa exigua* parasite latches on to a snapper fish's tongue and sucks its blood until the tongue atrophies and falls off. But instead of swimming on to its next victim, the parasite hooks itself into the fish where the tongue used to be and functions like a new tongue. The fish can use this new "tongue" just like its old one. The only difference is that the new tongue siphons off some of the fish's food. Sneaky and effective dieting technique, anyone?

SALTY WONDER

The world's greatest salt cave was discovered in Iran in 2006 by a team of researchers exploring other salt caves in the area. Measuring 6,580 meters (4.09 miles), the 3N cave is constantly changing shape, as rain streams cut some salt walls in half and create others with loose sediment. The cave, which resembles an ice palace in some areas, is home to beautiful and ever-changing salt sculptures and dripstones.

 ## POSSESSED CRABS

The female *Sacculina* parasite slips under a crab's armor and begins growing thin roots that snake through and around every part of the crab—even its eyestalks. Once her home is prepared, she makes room for the male *Sacculina* to join her. By the time the parasites are mating, the crab is completely enslaved by the parasites and spends all its energy doing their bidding.

THE STAMINA OF SQUIDS

A pair of squids starts having sex after a prolonged mating dance—and doesn't stop for two whole weeks.

They take breaks only so the female can dive to the ocean floor and deposit her eggs.

NO SWIMMING

The world's largest bioluminescent patch of ocean is the size of Connecticut and located off the horn of Africa. It wasn't discovered until 2005, when a scientist did some detective work and discovered the glowing area on satellite photos. Caused by bacteria *Vibrio harveyi*, this area, called "the milky sea," has long been the subject of rumor and speculation, especially in the sailing world.

METEORITE GRIEF

The first recorded instance of a celestial body hitting a human was in 1972, when Ann Elizabeth Hodges of Alabama was awoken by a meteoroid crashing into her living room as she napped. It smashed her radio and hit her on the arm. The event received attention around the world, and a legal battle, lasting a year, ensued over the humble rock. The U.S. Air Force, the Hodges, and the Hodges' landlord squabbled over who owned the meteorite, which was receiving offers of up to $5,000 from outer-space enthusiasts around the world. Ann Hodges eventually donated the meteorite to the University of Alabama, glad to have it out of her hair.

KLEPTOPARASITISM

Gulls in Florida land on pelicans and wait for them to open their mouths, then steal fish from their storage pouches. Ornithologists call this behavior *kleptoparasitism*.

THE HORRORS OF WHEAT

Everyone knows about the Salem Witch Trials, the 1692 superstition-fueled hysteria that left more than 20 dead and more than 100 accused of consorting with the devil. The fervor started when a couple of teenage girls demonstrated strange, hallucinatory behavior that the puritanical Salemers believed was connected to witchcraft. But what actually caused this behavior? Some historians believe that the unusually cold and wet 1692 winter produced moldy rye wheat, which contains the hallucination-inducing chemical ergot. Could it really have been something they ate?

When you were a tadpole
and I was a fish
In the Paleozoic time
And side by side on the ebbing tide
We sprawled through
the ooze and the slime . . ."
—LANGDON SMITH, *EVOLUTION*

RING OF FIRE

Johnny Cash single-handedly slashed the population of endangered California condors in the Los Padres National Wildlife Refuge from 53 to 9 when a gas leak in his car set fire to some grass. The blaze took two days to extinguish and required the efforts of 400 firemen, 4 helicopters, and 8 aerial tankers. Talk about a ring of fire. Thanks for nothing, Johnny Cash!

BULL'S EYE

Whether it's the erosion of a volcanic dome or a crater left by a hurtling asteroid, the Richat Structure, a bull's-eye-shaped indentation located in the middle of the Sahara desert, has been the subject of much debate. At more than 30 miles (48 km) wide, the structure, also called the Eye of Africa, is said to have been used as a landmark by early space travelers.

TREACHEROUS ORIGINS OF COMMON PLANT NAMES

From *The Dictionary of Plant Lore* by D. C. Watts and from *The Secrets of Wild Flowers* by Jack Sanders:

Forget-me-nots, *the small blue flowers at the side of the road, are so called because a young man who was picking them for his lover tumbled into a river and drowned. His parting cry to his love? "Forget me not!"*

The common red poppy is known as Blind Man *because it was believed that you would go blind if you rubbed it on your eyes.*

In medieval times, the Savin tree was nicknamed Bastard Killer *due to the powerful abortifacient properties of its fruit. Thomas Middleton alludes to this practice in his 1624 play* A Game of Chess: *"To gather fruit, find nothing but the savin-tree/Too frequent in nuns' orchards, and there planted/By all conjecture, to destroy fruit rather."*

The French word for dandelion is pissenlit (direct translation: "piss in the bed"). American and European folklore both hold that children who handle dandelions will wet the bed. In fact, dandelions contain a powerful natural diuretic, which just might push weak bladders over the edge.

The wild red trillium is sometimes called Stinking Benjamin because of its rotting-carrion stench. In times when people believed the scent or appearance of a plant indicated what it was good for, people used Stinking Benjamin to treat a stinky disease—gangrene.

The corpse plant, or Indian pipe, turns black and oozes a clear goo when picked. Said Alice Morse Earle, an American author writing at the turn of the nineteenth century, "It is the weirdest flower that grows, so palpably ghastly that we feel almost a cheerful satisfaction in the perfection of its performance and our own responsive thrill, just as we do in a good ghost story."

THE FRUIT OF REAL ESTATE

According to *The Dictionary of Plant Lore* by D. C. Watts, there was once an auction held in Somerset, England, at which one-acre plots of land were being sold. The plots were marked, and matching marks representing the plots were cut into apples. The apples were then put in a bag, and the land was allotted to the peasants by having them reach into the bag and grab an apple. That's one way to get around complicated land disputes!

ACORN EROTICA

Forget erect cacti and yonic blossoms this Valentine's Day. The acorn was one of the earliest phallic symbols. The acorn itself symbolizes the masculine, and the cup, the feminine. You can also determine whether or not your marriage will work out by putting an acorn and a cup in a bowl of water. If they float together, you'll be united for life. If they float apart, you're better off shaking a different tree.

ALMOND EROTICA

Scratch that—forget acorns this Valentine's Day. The almond takes the prize for the most sexual nut. In Greek mythology, Attis was castrated by the gods. He died, and his testicles fell to the ground, where an almond tree later sprouted. Nowadays, almonds are part of wedding ceremonies in Spain, Greece, Italy, and India because they are both bitter and sweet. In Greece, when an unmarried woman dies, almonds are served at the funeral to represent her marriage to God.

A WEED TO WATCH FOR

Europeans used to believe that bloody spots appeared on the leaves of St. John's wort plant on August 29, the anniversary of the saint's beheading. Not only that, people believed that if you happened to step on a St. John's wort plant, it would turn into a fairy horse that would run away with you on its back, depositing you miles away from home.

WONDERFUL WOLPHINS

A wolphin is a cross between a bottle-nosed dolphin and a killer whale. There are currently two female wolphins living in captvity at Hawaii's Sea Life Park, and the wondrous animals reportedly exist in the wild. In sea-faring lore, the wolphin is called "the great gray beast," and they grow to about 10 feet (3 m) in length:

exactly half the difference between the length of a dolphin and that of a killer whale. More remarkable still, they have 66 teeth: exactly 22 less than a dolphin's 88 teeth and 22 more than a killer whale's 44. Now do I play with it, or swim away screaming?

PIZZLY GROLAR

A pizzly is a cross between a polar bear and a grizzly bear, two genetically similar bears that typically avoid each other in the wild. A pizzly shot by an American hunter in Canada in 2006 was the first such bear to have been found in the wild. Way to go, *Dave*.

YOU COULD LITERALLY LOSE
A SMALL CHILD IN THIS PLANT

Rafflesia arnoldii is a parasitic plant with the world's largest bloom. The huge, red, bump-ridden petals stretch out to over 3 feet (about 1 meter) across, and the hole in the middle, where the pollen is, can hold 6 to 7 quarts (5.7 to 6.6 l) of water. It smells bad, and if you're not careful, you could probably lose a one-year-old or small dog inside this plant.

A SHAPELESS GENITAL BY ANY OTHER NAME . . .

The name of the towering *Amorphophallus* plant means literally "shapeless male genitalia." Come on guys, couldn't you have named it something nice, like "daisy"?

THE PURR OF DEATH

Oscar, a cat in a Rhode Island nursing home, can apparently sniff out imminent death among the elderly patients. Normally antisocial, Oscar will jump onto a patient's lap and nuzzle the person if he senses the end is near. The nursing staff have come to trust the cat's judgment, and call family members to tell them to make preparations when they spot a patient being nuzzled by Oscar. So far the cat has accurately predicted 24 deaths.

HE ROLLED SNAKE EYES

The former Guiness World Record holder for longest time spent in a cage with poisonous snakes was Trevor Kruger of South Africa, who remained with the reptiles for 36 days in 1975. Two weeks after coming out of the cage, he was killed in a car accident. In 2006, Kruger's record was broken by 25-year-old Peter Snyman, who stayed in a cage with 24 puff adders, Egyptian cobras, black mambas, and South African boomslangs for 50 consecutive days.

I LOVE CHEESE, REAAAALLY I DO

The holes in Swiss cheese are created by expansion of gas in the cheese curd during the ripening process. They're also called "eyes."

WINE FOR THE HARDY

Instructions for "eskimo wine," found on the Internet: "Put a seagull in a bottle. Fill with water. Let it ferment in the sun." Mazeltov!

INVISIBLE INK FOR BEES

Many flowers have patterns called "honey guides," which point bees to the flower's nectar. Humans can see most of these patterns with the naked eye. The evening primrose, however, looks yellow to humans; though insects can see and follow the honey guide, humans can see it only under ultraviolet light.

ANIMAL SYMBOLS

- In East Indian mythology, the dog is the vehicle of departing souls.

- In Roman mythology, a tiger skin is the token of Bacchus, god of revelry.

- In Egyptian mythology, the bull is an emblem of the god of creativity.

- In Russian symbolism, a horse represents marriage and happy homemaking.

- In Japan, wild geese flying represent manhood, and fireflies represent fallen warriors.

- In Chinese mythology, five bats together represent wealth, longevity, health, love of virtue, and a peaceful end.

- In ancient Egypt, the sphinx represented intelligence and strength. But in ancient Greece, it represented secrecy and pestilence!

Symbolism was the genius of the Egyptian nation.
—CHARLES LENORMANT

11. BRIDE OF THE BIZARRE

WACKY WEDDINGS, TRAGIC NUPTIALS,
RITUAL ORIGINS, AND ODD COUPLES

If I must die,
I will encounter darkness as a bride,
And hug it in my arms

—WILLIAM SHAKESPEARE, *MEASURE FOR MEASURE*

IS IT REALLY LEGAL TO MARRY A ROCK OR A pillow? Is there any rhyme or reason to wedding traditions? Like the Bride of Frankenstein, this chapter is a continuation of what I think of as the key to the story—or in this case, to bizarre trivia—of how absolutely odd people really are. Some of the facts contained in this chapter might make you rethink your wedding plans. Who needs the traditional church aisle when you can get married on the wings of a bi-plane? And because I am a lover of the morbid kind, I couldn't resist a few wedding-day ghosts and horrifying deaths to round it out. Till death do us part, after all!

PICKING UP THE PIECES

In Germany, there is a tradition of shattering large numbers of dishes before the wedding and having the bride and groom clean up the pieces.

Farewell, dear wife! my life is past;
I loved you while my life did last;
Don't grieve for me, or sorrow take,
But *love my brother* for my sake.
—EPITAPH IN A CHURCHYARD AT SARATOGA

KISS OFF

At wedding receptions in Sweden, there is a kissing custom that is certainly not for the jealous type! If the bride leaves the room, all the women line up to kiss the groom, and if the groom leaves, the men do the same for the bride. (No word on what happens when the bride or groom return.)

An old Irish tradition was for wedding couples to dine on salt and oats at the beginning of their wedding reception, to ward off the evil eye.

TILL DEATH DO US PART

In June 2009, in the picturesque town of Soledad, California, a 26-year-old woman collapsed at her wedding reception. The victim of an unpredictable brain aneurysm, she died that day—her wedding day.

LORD OF THE RING

More than one year after his wedding ring fell from his finger into the sea, a New Zealand man recovered the symbol of his love. When it slipped from his finger and sank to the bottom of the sea, Aleki Taumoepeau, who had then been married only three months, did not lose all hope. He roughly marked the spot and pledged that he would find it. Using satellite coordinates and a prayer, he arranged a dive back in the spot where he believed it had disappeared. After searching for about an hour (and a year), he spotted the ring shining through the waters.

Lend me a looking-glass; If that her breath will mist or stain the stone. Why then, she lives.
—WILLIAM SHAKESPEARE, *KING LEAR*

PRACTICING RESTRAINT

A man in Batavia, New York was arrested on his wedding day for violating a court-issued restraining order— by going near his bride. The bride, who was also the man's ex-wife, had previously had a restraining order against him. When the man got into an argument with one of the wedding guests, officers were called in to settle the dispute. The police recognized the man from previous arrests and discovered the restraining order was still active. They arrested him on criminal contempt. The real question is, what was she thinking?

———— ◄►► ————

Queen Victoria made the white wedding gown fashionable. When marrying Prince Albert in 1840, she wore a pale gown adorned with orange blossoms. A trend was set.

Here lies my wife, a sad slattern and shrew,
If I said I regretted her, I should lie too!
—EPITAPH ON A GRAVE AT SELBY, YORKSHIRE, ENGLAND

BEYOND BIZARRE

WINGS OF LOVE

Katie Hodgson and her groom, Darren McWalters, strapped themselves to the wings of identical biplanes, which flew side by side about 1,000 feet above ground, and recited their wedding vows. The reverend who married them used airborne communications to perform the ceremony.

The role of best man was originally that of an armed guard—in case the bride needed to be kidnapped away from disapproving parents.

PROTECTIVE DRESS

Bridesmaids' dresses were not originally the punishment they are today (think pink taffeta you will never wear again). They served a very practical purpose: a bride's attendants were told to dress in a gown similar to that of the bride so that as her party walked to the church, she wouldn't be easily recognized by evil spirits or by jealous would-be suitors. The same applied to the groomsmen dressing like the groom.

AND THE BRIDE WORE BLACK

There is a Scottish prenuptial tradition of blackening the bride, in which the bride is essentially tarred and feathered. She is kidnapped by her friends, covered in anything gooey or foul, such as honey, eggs, sauce and feathers, and then dragged about on a pub crawl.

The organ pealed forth . . . In every heart begat to spring that exquisite hope, seldom if ever realized, that the bride will have had a fit, or eloped with someone else.
—ANGELA THIRKELL, *CHEERFUL BREAKS IN*

It is against the law in North Carolina to register at a hotel as a married couple if you aren't actually married.

WEDDING-DAY CURSE

According to the website *Britain.tv*, there are numerous weird and wacky wedding stories. But the most tragic is the story of the son of the king of Italy and his ill-fated wedding day. In 1867, Princess Maria del Pozzo della Cisterno married the Duke D'Aosta, son of Italy's king. On their wedding day, the princess's wardrobe mistress hung herself, the gatekeeper at the palace cut his own throat, the stationmaster was killed beneath the honeymoon train, the leader of the wedding procession collapsed from heatstroke, the king's aide died after falling from his horse, and the best man shot himself.

SWEPT OFF HER FEET

When a young man in Oregon planned his romantic proposal, he hadn't accounted for the sneaky wave that would sweep his bride-to-be off to sea. Scott Napper and his late girlfriend, Leafil Alfoque, were heading to Proposal Rock, with the ring in his pocket, when a three-foot wave knocked the petite Alfoque off of her feet and dragged her out to sea. She disappeared and was presumed drowned.

The first wedding to occur in the White House was that of Miss Todd, a relative by marriage of President James Madison.

Diamonds were once believed to protect their wearer from evil spirits and maintain concord between husband and wife. For these reasons, the diamond has become a traditional inset in a wedding ring.

Marriage by capture is the oldest way of starting a new family.

Gather ye rosebuds while ye may,
Old Time is still a-flying,
And this same flower that smiles to-day
To-morrow will be dying.
—ROBERT HERRICK,
"TO THE VIRGINS, TO MAKE MUCH OF TIME"

The practice of tying shoes to the bumper of the newlyweds' car is believed to have developed from the old English practice of throwing shoes at the groom—supposedly for taking the bride away.

WHY THE THIRD FINGER ON THE LEFT?

Placing the wedding ring on the third finger of the left hand has its origins in a Grecian belief that a vein ran directly from the heart to that finger.

VEIN OF LOVE

The practice of wearing engagement rings on the fourth finger of the left hand dates back to the ancient Egyptians, who believed there was a "vein of love" running from this finger to the heart.

SPUN GOLD

In what may possibly be the most elaborate wedding in history, Charles Durande, a wealthy slave owner in Louisiana, decorated his yard in a most unusual and extravagant manner. In anticipation of the wedding of his two daughters, he ordered a shipload of spiders from China, which he released into the trees around his plantation. When the thousands of arachnids had spun thousands of webs, Durande's slaves, using hand-operated bellows, coated the webs with gold and silver dust, which he had imported from the mines of California. The 2,000 people in attendance were reportedly impressed.

FIRST COMES LOVE, THEN COMES MARRIAGE

The concept of the stork bringing the baby has its roots in the very natural nesting habits of Scandinavian storks. Early ornithologists observed that storks often built their nests on chimneystacks. This position allowed people a bird's eye view of their habits, which included monogamy and the care and feeding of children and elders. From these observations evolved the tale of a gentle and caring creature dropping a new bundle of joy down the chimney. Hans Christian Andersen popularized the concept, and it spread.

FRANCISCAN FLORA

The ghost of Flora Sommerton, who disappeared one evening in 1876, has appeared to visitors of San Francisco. Most often spotted near an apartment house near the Fairmount Hotel in the Nob Hill district, she appears in her bridal gown, a woman walking quickly as if to get away from someone or something. The story goes that Sommerton did not wish to marry the man her parents had chosen for her, and she fled. She was never seen again by her mother or father, and she reportedly died in a flophouse in Montana, still wearing her bridal gown. Her ghost appears most often late at night or early in the morning.

In 2009, Ryanair, the Irish airline that offers cheap flights to and from Ireland and mainland Europe, issued its own baggage restrictions. Brides whose wedding dress will not fit in the overhead bin need to book an extra seat for the dress!

VOWS, SHMOWS

In 2009, a Saudi groom on his honeymoon boarded the plane back from Malaysia to Saudi Arabia without his bride, who he said was in the restroom and taking too long. He allowed the flight to leave without her. She insisted on an immediate divorce.

A wedding ring should never be removed unless it is being used to ward off a witch.

The bitterest creature under heaven if the wife who discovers that her husband's bravery is only bravado, that his strength is only a uniform, that is power is but a gun in the hands of a fool. —PEARL S. BUCK, *LOVE AND MARRIAGE*

SATAN'S SATIN

The substance of a bride's dress extends beyond color. Silk is believed to be the material of the most fortune, whereas velvet can bring poverty, and satin is simply bad luck.

CAKE HOLE

An old custom of spousal divination suggests a young girl should take a bit of wedding cake, pass it through a wedding ring, and then place the cake in her left stocking. The stocking should be placed under her pillow that night, where it will cause the would-be bride to dream of her future husband.

The Romans considered May the most unlucky month for weddings, as it was the month they dedicated to celebrating the dead.

BAD OMENS

During the Middle Ages, if anyone in the bridal party came across any of the following on their way to the church, it was an omen of ill luck: a monk, a priest, a dog, a lizard, a hare, a snake

If anyone came across a spider, toad, or wolf, however, it was considered great luck!

SOMETHING OLD, SOMETHING NEW, SOMETHING SOMEONE SAID IS TRUE!

The phrase "something old, something new, something borrowed, and something blue" has been chanted to brides for centuries. And brides have been donning their mother's pearls and sliding on their brand-new blue garters for centuries too, but not everyone knows the symbolism of these traditional items. It is said that a bride must wear something old to provide her with security. Something new will ensure good luck and happiness. Something borrowed should be borrowed from a woman who wore it at a time of great happiness. And finally, something blue represents the purity and divinity of the blue sky and is believed to protect the bride from jealousy and negativity.

LET THEM SLEEP ON CAKE!

The bride should place a piece of wedding cake under the marriage bed to ensure faithfulness.

WHAT ABOUT EIGHT TIMES?

You can break the curse of "thrice a bridesmaid, never a bride" by being a bridesmaid seven times.

LIPS FOR DAYS

The average person spends 20,160 minutes kissing over their lifetime. Better stock up on breath mints!

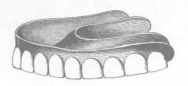

RECOMMENDED BY THE AMERICAN DENTAL ASSOCIATION

Feel a cavity coming on? Find someone to make out with. The extra saliva you get from kissing has been shown to help prevent tooth decay.

NEWBORN NUPTUALS

In late 2007, the state of Arkansas accidentally amended state law to allow persons of any age to get married with parental permission. Lawmakers realized their mistake and corrected the law in April 2008. Statistics are unavailable on how many three-year-olds tied the knot in the intervening period.

To marry a woman you love and who loves you is to lay a wager with her as to who will stop loving the other first.
—ALFRED CAPUS, *NOTES ET PENSÉES*

LOVE IS COLOR-BLIND

In 1918, the Imperial Household Ministry of Japan tried to call off the wedding of 14-year-old Princess Nagako to Prince Hirohito of Japan after discovering that color-blindness ran in Princess Nagako's family. Her father, Prince Kuni, refused to withdraw his daughter from the marriage and said that if the imperial court broke the engagement, he would avenge his honor by stabbing both his daughter and himself to death. After a nationwide scandal, the imperial court allowed the wedding to proceed.

AN UNUSUAL WEDDING GIFT

Star of the big screen Joan Crawford was no stranger to the altar—or to the bathroom section of Home Depot. Each time she got married, she changed all the toilet seats in her house.

FREAKY WEDDING BELIEFS

- The first spouse to fall asleep on the wedding night will be the first to die.

- Meeting a nun or monk on the wedding day is an omen of barrenness.

HANDY STANDING

In Christian marriages, the groom stands to the right of the bride so that he has ready access to his sword to fight off rival suitors.

Marriage is a good deal like a circus: there is not as much in it as represented in the advertising. —EDGAR WATSON HOWE, *COUNTRY TOWN SAYINGS*

NICE DAY FOR A WHITE FUNERAL

In reaction to the numerous "freak requests" he had from women wanting to be buried in their wedding dresses, an undertaker wrote in 1910, "These gowns look awfully old fashioned and have a musty odor appropriately suggestive of the grave, after having been done up in lavender and tissue paper for so many years, but vanity no longer plays a part in the scheme of the old ladies' existence, and style is to them a small matter compared with the gratification of sentiment." But the women were no match for one man, who requested to be buried in a sheet, saying, "I am going to do a good deal of haunting when I'm through with the flesh, and I'm going to take the sheet along with me so there will be no delay about getting down to business."

Superstitious brides and grooms plan their wedding in the month of June, which is said to be the luckiest month for nuptials—possibly because, in the northern hemisphere, it's the month with the best weather. In Poland, only the months with the letter *r* in them are said to be propitious for weddings.

The tradition of brides wearing veils on their wedding day may be derived from the Eastern practice of *purdah,* which forbade a man from seeing his future wife's face until they were married. Another theory is that the veil is worn to protect the bride against the evil eye.

THOSE TWO BETTER STAY TOGETHER

The award for most ridiculously lavish wedding of all time might go to Rashid bin Sayid al-Maktoum, sheik of Dubai, who spent more than $44 million on his son's wedding to Princess Salama in 1981. The party went on for 7 nights, was attended by 20,000 guests, and took place in a stadium built expressly for the event.

Fat lady Hannah Perkins, made famous by performing with P. T Barnum's circus and weighing approximately 700 lbs, was the unlikely wife of John Battersby, who performed in the same circus as a "living skeleton" and weighed an astonishing 45 lbs. Similarly, Pete Robinson of the Ringling Brothers' circus, who weighed only 58 lbs, was married to his fellow performer, fat lady Bunny Smith, who weighed in at 467 lbs, in a ceremony that took place at Madison Square Garden.

PILLOW TALK

In March of 2010, a 28-year-old South Korean man married a pillow. The body pillow, which has an anime character printed on one side, was dressed in a white wedding dress. Ever the gentleman, the groom reportedly takes the pillow out to regular dinner (ordering "her" a meal) and even brought the pillow with him to an amusement park.

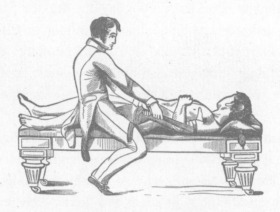

JEALOUS JAILBIRDS

In early March of 2010, a couple spent their first night as newlyweds in a rather unattractive honeymoon suite—a Massachusetts jail. The bride was arrested after trying to run over her groom's ex in a parking lot. Her groom was by her side—and a passenger in the car. Both were arrested, and the bride was charged with assault and battery with a deadly weapon. The groom was charged with disorderly conduct, and both were booked into separate cells in the local jail. They were released the next day.

12. THERE'S BLOOD IN THEM THAR HILLS!

GHOST TOWNS, LOST CEMETERIES, AND MORE TRUE GHOST ENCOUNTERS

The four boards of the coffin lid
Heard all the dead man did.
—ALGERNON CHARLES SWINBURNE, "AFTER DEATH"

I GREW UP IN A GOLD RUSH TOWN IN CALIFORNIA where it was common practice to spend time walking through the remains of what once were miner's cabins fallen to the wild brush and pines, solitary graves alongside roads that once led wagons toward the promise of riches. The abandoned and the preserved, the hidden and the haunted. Because of course, where there are ghost towns, there are ghosts. And where there are ghosts, there are stories . . .

ANCIENT WONDERS

We haven't seen them all yet! In November 2008, an Egyptian archaeologist announced the discovery of a 4,300-year-old pyramid in Saqqara, once known as the ancient city of Memphis, located about twelve miles south of Cairo. According to Egypt's chief archaeologist, the pyramid is believed to belong to Queen Sesheshet, who lived during the Sixth Dynasty.

Ever held a Dead Man's Hand? In poker, a pair of aces is referred to by this term. Why? When Wild Bill Hickock was killed—shot in the back—he was playing poker, and in his hand he held two aces.

The Grave yields back her Robberies—
The Years, our pilfered Things—
Bright Knots of Apparitions—
Salute us, with their wings

—EMILY DICKINSON,
"OF NEARNESS TO HER SUNDERED THINGS"

KEEP YOUR EYES PEELED

In *Coast to Coast Ghosts*, Leslie Rule describes the five most common places to see an apparition:

1. Peering out of windows

2. On staircases

3. In hallways

4. Perched in chairs

5. In mirrors

IT'S STILL A JUNGLE OUT THERE

A tract forest in western Brazil, once believed to be virgin forest, revealed signs of an extensive human settlement, including signs of farming, wetland management, dams, walls, human-waste dumps, and fish farms, as well as evidence of a network of roads arranged around a large central plaza. *Science Journal* reported in late August 2009 that the population was most likely wiped out by diseases brought by the early European colonists in the 15th century. Who exactly populated the villages and central community—which covers nearly 150 acres—is still a mystery.

TAKE ME WITH YOU

In São Paulo, Brazil, a woman was killed by the coffin of her own husband. In November 2008, 67-year-old Marciana Silva Barcelos was riding in the passenger seat of the hearse that was carrying her husband's coffin to the cemetery when a traffic accident caused the coffin to lurch forward and strike her in the back of the neck, killing her instantly.

DEATHLY WORDS

The following are the deathbed words of a few famous folks:

- Benjamin Franklin: "A dying man can do nothing easy."

- Lord Byron: "I must sleep now."

- George Sand: *"Laissez la verdure."* ("Leave the tomb green.")

- Demonax (the philosopher): "You may go home, the show is over."

- Lord Elden: "It matters not, where I am going, whether the weather be cold or hot."

RING ME WHEN YOU WAKE

In Penny Colman's book *Corpses, Coffins, and Crypts: A History of Burial,* she describes the extremes that people have gone to in order to ensure that they were not buried alive. At the West Point Cemetery in Highland Falls, New York, there stands a replica of an ancient Egyptian pyramid. The pyramid, known as the Viele

Memorial, contains the remains of Egbert Ludovicus Viele, whose fear of premature burials was so great that he arranged to have a buzzer placed inside the memorial that was connected to the caretaker's house and would ring there, should Viele find himself alive inside his own memorial. When he died in 1902, his body was placed inside a sarcophagus. The buzzer never rang and is now disconnected.

Viele's fear is not all that irrational. There are many cases of premature burial. Colman describes several, including the tale of Philomele Jonetre, who was buried in the 1860s in a cemetery in Paris when people walking by heard a tapping coming from her grave. The coroner exhumed her body and found her eyelids moving. She revived, but died (again) the next day.

NO AMOUNT OF MONEY WILL SAVE YOU FROM THIS

Anwar Rashid purchased a 52-room mansion, known as Clifton Hall and located in Yorkshire, England. But eight months later, he and this family moved out, and he stopped paying the mortgage. Why? Because it was haunted. Rashid said that during the months that he and his family lived there, they repeatedly heard unexplained noises—tapping, voices—and saw shadowy figures. Rashid, a skeptic when it comes to the paranormal, reported that they left after finding blood-red spots on their baby's blanket. About the mysterious mansion, he said, "I would have to tell any new owner that it was haunted, having experienced it." Rashid paid £3.6 million for the mansion, but in the end, the money he lost was not enough to convince him to stay.

THE OLD CUCHILLO BAR

The Old Cuchillo Bar in Cuchillo, New Mexico (a ghost town just outside of Albuquerque), is reputed to be one of the most haunted places in the Southwest. Once a stagecoach stop, it has been the site of many mysterious events—whispers from unseen people, objects falling without cause, the sound of the woodstove being opened and wood being stacked by disembodied hands. The bar's current owner, Josh Bond, was so taken by the many activities that he called in the West Coast Ghost and Paranormal Society, as well as Ghost Investigations New Mexico, to investigate the old adobe compound, which includes an old hotel and saloon. You can visit the Old Cuchillo Bar's website (*www.cuchillobar.com*) to find history, access links to electronic-voice phenomenon (EVP) recordings, and arrange a stay.

BODIE BEWITCHED

One of the most fascinating ghost towns in the West, Bodie, California was once the second-biggest city in all of California. Nestled high in the Sierras at more than 8,000 feet above sea level, Bodie's long winters keep most visitors away until the summer. But some residents remain indefinitely—the ghosts. Ghostly music, banging and hammering, the frightening ghost of an Asian woman who appears in an upstairs window and once pushed someone down the stairs—nearly every house in Bodie is reputed to be haunted. During the summer, Bodie hosts more than 200,000 visitors who come to see the empty bar stools, the abandoned bottles, the slow decay of a town that is the epitome of ghostly. Whether you believe in the haunting or you simply love history, a trip to this town is worth its weight in gold.

THREE TIMES

Author Lisa Rogak writes about funeral traditions from around the world in *Death Warmed Over*. She describes the Mongolian custom of burial as taking place within 24 hours of death; in this custom, the head of the deceased always needs to face south. Rogak continues, "Once the body is found, family and guests walk around the grave three times, pouring the fermented milk of a horse around the perimeter, ostensibly to fortify the soul for its impending journey."

Hereto I come to view a voiceless ghost;
Whither, O whither will its whim now draw me?
—THOMAS HARDY, "AFTER A JOURNEY"

 ## BUTCHERTOWN, U.S.A.

The San Francisco neighborhood known today as Bayview was once known as Butchertown, because it was home to slaughterhouses. They were so numerous that it is said the nearby Islais Creek ran red with blood.

In a similar fashion, Louisville, Kentucky's own Butchertown was once home to butchers and stockyards. Their location was chosen because of its proximity to a creek, where animal remains were tossed. At the time, this unsanitary practice was banned from the more populated downtown districts, making the outlying areas perfect places for such disposal.

In Chicago's Graceland Cemetery, staring into the eyes of the statue of a tall, robed figure of the monument known as "Eternal Silence" is said to give one visions of one's own death.

ROCK OUT WITH YOUR GHOST OUT

No ghost hunter's tour of Charlottesville, Virginia, is complete without a visit to two historic haunts: Ash Lawn, the historic home to former president James Monroe, and neighboring Monticello, the estate of former president Thomas Jefferson.

At Ash Lawn, reports of a haunted chair have spanned the decades. Countless visitors have testified to having seen a rocking chair in the main room rock all on its own.

At Monticello, the apparition of Thomas Jefferson himself is rumored to have been seen, most often around the little honeymoon cottage behind the main house, where Jefferson's many infidelities are thought to have taken place.

A PLEASANT SMELL

Clairalience or clairescence is the term used in parapsychology for the extra-sensory perception of something paranormal by means of scent or smelling. Rickey Turner, a Mt. Pleasant, Tennessee man, experienced this very phenomenon.

My mother passed away with terminal cancer in September, 1993 at the age of 58. My three sisters and I gave her care during her sickness. She passed away at her home, which was her request.

My mother was a very dignified lady. There was a certain perfume that she liked which was called "Passion." About a week after my mother had died, my eldest sister told me that one day she felt a very strong presence of my mother. When she felt it, she also smelled the perfume. I sort of dismissed it and really didn't give it much thought.

I was working the evening shift at a plant that produces graphite and coal electrodes for the steel industry. I work in the production department. It was about two weeks since my mother had passed away. I worked in a building that has furnaces that would bake these coal and graphite electrodes. Naturally the building is full of fumes such as natural gas, coal fumes, etc. The building itself is constructed so that the furnace air will rise up through the building and go out the vented roof. Even the building walls are vented to allow the dust and fumes to escape.

During my shift that afternoon I was to unload a furnace. I was standing on the walkway that goes around each of the furnaces, unloading as usual. All of a sudden there came an aroma of perfume all around me. I called another employee over and asked him if he smelled anything. He told me he could smell something perfumey in the air. We stood there for several minutes while the perfume odor remained. He finally went back to his job station. Anywhere I walked on the furnace, the perfume odor remained. The perfume remained with me for about 20 minutes, and then it disappeared.

Oh, one more thing. My oldest daughter experienced the same thing. That makes three now.

Thanks again to Rickey for sharing this amazing story!

STONE COLD

The origin of the tombstone lies in the fear of the dead, it seems. Lest the restless spirit, zombie, or other ghastly incarnation of the formerly living try to escape from its well-nailed coffin and six feet of earthly barrier, a large heavy stone was added to the grave to ensure it was sealed. Later, the tombstone was used more formally as a place on which to engrave epitaphs and depict angels, doves, and similar symbols of heavenly ascension.

The ticking wood-worm mocks thee, man!
—THOMAS CAMPBELL, "HALLOWED GROUND"

TWICE DEAD IN WISCONSIN

In 1925, a few miles south of Portage, Wisconsin, August and Patricia Heinz and their children suffered trauma of the supernatural variety. The family, which also included 7-year-old Freddy, 9-year-old Charles, and 11-year-old Elizabeth, had moved into the simple two-story farmhouse 10 years before and lived there happily, without incident. But then, in February 1925, an unexplained fire destroyed one of the barns. In June, another barn burned, also without explanation. And then late one June evening, as the family sat down to supper, they heard the sound of footsteps descending from the second floor. Young Charles and his father investigated, but found no one else in the home. After they had sat back down with the rest of the family, the footsteps began again. This phantom sound continued on and off for the next three months.

Further incidents began to occur. Patricia discovered that each morning her broom was missing from the kitchen, only to turn up in some strange place, such as a remote corner of the property or a different room in the house. Suspecting the children up to mischief, August and Patricia questioned each one, but all insisted they had nothing to do with it. Exasperated, Patricia decided to chain down the broom and lock the kitchen door. The next morning, she was horrified to discover the door still locked, but the chain broken and the broom outside in the yard.

The events culminated one evening when August and his neighbor returned from a hunting trip. Once everyone, including their guest, were seated at the table, the sound of footsteps began. August recounted the story of this mysterious ghost to their guest. The neighbor decided to take action. Thinking that he might scare the ghost, he took his unloaded shotgun and crept toward the stairs where the sound of footsteps had been heard. He leapt out, let forth a wild scream, and pointed his gun. Though he believed the gun to be unloaded, a shot flew out, shattering the plaster and wallpaper. Freddy and Charles recalled hearing a moan after the shot, and all the family members heard the sounds of moans and cries coming from the fruit cellar. Once the sounds had ceased, the family was never again haunted by the spirit of the house.

I look for ghosts; but none will force
Their way to me: 'tis falsely said
That there was ever intercourse
Between the living and the dead
—WILLIAM WORDSWORTH,
"THE AFFLICTION OF MARGARET"

AFTERLIFE ELITE

The historic town of Rugby, located in Big South Fork in the mountains of Tennessee, was once a thriving community of highbrowed Englishman. It was founded in 1880 by Thomas Hughes, but his vision of an educated and refined community in the backwoods of Tennessee came to fruition only briefly. Fires and the typhoid epidemic wiped out the population, but left behind many interesting ghosts. These include a German librarian who wanders the library, a snoring ghost in the cottage of Thomas Hughes, and a wailing woman in the Roslyn House. In addition, visitors to this literal ghost town have heard the sounds of horse and carriage. Adding to its bewitching appeal to seekers of the strange is a hiking trail that begins at the historic Laurel Dale cemetery, where many of the former residents of Rugby are buried.

ALMOST SAVED

The story of the Donner Party is legendary: crossing the Sierras in the winter of 1846–7, short on food, and long on miles, members of the party resorted to eating their deceased. And in a gruesome twist, this ill-fated group was nearly spared further loss. As related by local archeologist C. Ward, and based on a few documents regarding the history of the Paiute—the tribe local to the Sierras near Bear Valley, California:

On a cold and mournful day in November of 1846, the Donner Party was almost saved. The Paiute, who had been following and watching the Donner Party for a number of days, were preparing to intervene. They carried with them animal skin blankets, caches of pine nuts and dried fish, all to offer in aide for the struggling party. But as they watched from a hillside just above the clearing of the meadow at Bear Valley, which is now marked as the Pioneer Immigrant Trail, the Paiute bore witness to something that made them turn back. They witnessed the party begin to excavate the bodies of the fallen members previously buried in the snow, and then harvest the flesh for consumption. According to accounts, one Paiute said, "We cannot help them any longer." And the Paiute turned away. The Donner Party, who would cannibalize one more party member, and who would suffer more than 40 deaths, would eventually descend the slopes of the Sierras to the town of Nevada City.

You can still visit this spot today. Head east on Highway 20 outside of Nevada City for approximately 26 miles to the big valley that lies about one mile west of Bowman Lake Road. Hidden in the trees at the northern edge of the meadow and small valley is a small monument to the Pioneer Immigrant Trail. To picture the vantage point of the Paiute, look up into the hills of the northeast and imagine what they bore witness to.

And each separate dying ember wrought its ghost upon the floor. —EDGAR ALLAN POE, "THE RAVEN"

DEAD OR ALIVE

According to the Associated Press, there was a bizarre burglary in April 2008 in Spain. A prowler broke into a funeral home in Burjassot (no one is sure exactly what the burglar intended to steal), and when neighbors alerted police, the creepy criminal tried to hide. Police, along with the funeral parlor's owner, searched the place and found him lying on a table in a glassed-in viewing chamber that is used during wakes. The police said not only was he breathing, but he was also dressed shabbily—a dead giveaway in a parlor where the custom is to dress the deceased in their finest suits.

THE POE VISITOR

For more than 60 years, on January 19, the birthday of Edgar Allan Poe, a mystery visitor has slipped into the Baltimore graveyard housing Poe's remains and left roses and a bottle of cognac on the poet's grave. But January 19, 2010, marked the first time since 1949 that Poe House and Museum curator Jeff Jerome didn't see the familiar gifts left below the poet's gravestone. The infamous "Poe Toaster" usually arrived between midnight and 5:30 a.m. and sometimes laid his hands on the grave in a gesture of respect (according to unobtrusive onlookers, who have also made a tradition of visiting the grave on that day). Perhaps the original Poe Toaster has passed on. Will another Poe lover carry on the tradition?

GETTYSBURG GHOSTS

Ghost enthusiasts have long debated what is the most haunted town in America, and a growing number of them claim it's Gettysburg, Pennsylvania, where the famous Battle of Gettysburg took place on July 1, 1863. Fifty-one thousand men died there that day, and a couple of them are bound to have stuck around for some good old-fashioned hauntin', right?

The "Devil's Den" is said to be the most haunted of the Gettysburg battlefield sites. A rocky enclave providing perfect cover for a sharpshooter to hide and take out unsuspecting soldiers, the den was also a great place for photographers. It is said that a photographer by the name of Alexander Gardner, at the site directly after the battle ended, dragged a fallen soldier into the den to make it appear as if the corpse was that of the sharpshooter. But the ghost of a man who's been moved from his place of death is said to be active and angry, and modern-day picture-takers find the area around the den particularly inhospitable for taking pictures; their shots don't come out, the light is bad, and their shutters stick.

Just one civilian died at the Battle of Gettysburg—a woman named Jennie Wade, who was hit by a stray bullet that entered her house at the very beginning of the battle. Wade and her father, who went insane and was institutionalized after Jennie's death, are said to roam the house where they once lived.

The Farnsworth House, constructed by John McFarland in 1833, housed many Confederate sharpshooters during the battle. To this day, its south-side wall is riddled with more than a hundred Civil War bullets. The house is said to be haunted by a ghost named Mary, who sits with sick inn visitors, and the ghosts of rebel soldiers, who move trunks back and forth in the attic. The ghost of a soldier who died in that attic is supposedly the source of blood running down the shower walls in the bathroom below.

The tourist attraction the Chinese call "Ghost City" is, in reality, on its way to becoming one. The Three Gorges dam project, a hydroelectric river dam currently being built along the Yangtze River, will soon be completed, submerging the Taoist spiritual town of Fengdu in the process. But more than just the town will be lost: Fengdu has for centuries been the site of more than 75 Taoist temples and statues and is known as a Taoist graveyard. Taoists believe that super beings of the spirit world live in the temples, and the spirits of hundreds of thousands of people go there when they die. When the dam project submerges those temples in water, where will the spirits go?

A GHOST OF A HOTEL

When the grand, lavish Goldfield Hotel in Goldfield, Nevada, opened at the turn of the 19th century, it boasted more than 150 rooms with such modern conveniences as telephones and electricity. By the 1930s, the Goldfield began to lose business with the decline of gold mining. During World War II, it was home to U.S. Army Air Corps personnel, but was abandoned after the war. Today, the Goldfield lives on as a home to many ghosts; in fact, several psychics have named it one of "seven doors" to another world.

One of the hotel's ghosts is that of a prostitute named Elizabeth, who was supposedly murdered by the original owner of the hotel. Afraid the pregnant girl would ruin his reputation, legend has it that he locked her in room 109 and chained her to a radiator. Once born, her baby was thrown down a mineshaft, and Elizabeth was murdered soon after. It is said Elizabeth still haunts the halls in search of her child, whose cries can be heard throughout the building. Complaints of extreme cold in room 109 were often reported, and a reporter from Las Vegas claims he once took a photograph in the room and captured an image of Elizabeth chained to the radiator.

HAUNTED CEMETERIES: BUT A FEW

There are, quite literally, thousands of haunted cemeteries across the United States, not to mention the world. Here are but a few of the U.S. stops one must make on a haunted-cemetery tour. For one of the most complete listings, pick up a copy of Troy Taylor's *Field Guide to Haunted Graveyards*.

Kinston, Alabama: Harrison Cemetery is haunted by an old square dancer. Visitors have reported hearing lively fiddle music coming from his tomb.

Fairbanks, Alaska: Birch Hill Cemetery is home to the ghost of a young woman in a white dress, perhaps the daughter of a pioneer or early miner.

Colma, California: The Pioneer Cemetery is said to be haunted by the ghost of a woman wearing a burgundy dress and her gray hair pulled back into a bun. She watches over the Scheiffer plot.

St. Augustine, Florida: The Huguenot Cemetery, one of the oldest cemeteries in the United States, is supposedly one of the most haunted. A headless specter wanders among the graves. It is thought to be the ghost of a deceased occupant whose tomb was vandalized and whose head was stolen.

Justice, Illinois: Located just outside of Chicago, the Archer Woods Cemetery is said to be haunted by a weeping woman in white, most often spotted flagging down cars at night, as well as a phantom, driverless hearse pulled by a team of horses and carrying an illuminated child's coffin.

Gladstone, Michigan: The North Bluff Cemetery is haunted by the ghost of a woman in a white bridal gown.

Lakefield, Minnesota: Loon Lake Cemetery, an often overlooked and remote graveyard, is haunted by the ghosts of three witches who were buried there in the 1800s, as well as by many other spirits. Beware! There is a legend that if you walk over the grave of one of the witches, known as Mary Jane, you will soon die.

13. STRANGE AMERICA

CREEPY COLLECTIONS, ODD MUSEUMS,
AND AMERICANS BEHAVING WEIRDLY

When you're born into this world, you're given
a ticket to the freak show. If you're born in America,
you get a front row seat. —GEORGE CARLIN

ONE THING WE KNOW IS TRUE: TRUTH IS STRANGER than fiction. And the good ol' U.S. of A. is home to some of the strangest and absurd truths. Bizarre museums, outlandish collections, and all manner of attractions from sea to shining sea—here are just few of the many places, people, and things I have encountered in my travels across this nation of the strange.

OUR LADY OF THE GRIDDLE

A restaurant in Calexico, California, received a surge of fame when the likeness of the Virgin Mary appeared on its griddle. The Las Palmas removed the griddle from its place between the burners and set up a shrine in a storage room, for all to visit.

Embalming became a common funerary practice during the Civil War, when bodies needed to be shipped long distances to the families of dead soldiers.

BOOK HER

Twenty-year-old Heidi Dalibor of Grafton, Wisconsin, was arrested and booked for failure to pay her library fines. When she didn't respond to calls and letters requesting payment of fines and return of the books *White Oleander* and *Angels and Demons*, local police issued a warrant for her arrest. She was handcuffed, fingerprinted, and photographed, and she remained in custody until her bail was paid.

Between 1940 and 2003, just over 9,000 people were killed by lightning in the United States.

EVIDENCE SWALLOWING FOR THE NEW MILLENNIUM

A New York City man being questioned by U.S. government agents for some kind of identity theft scheme dramatically seized and swallowed the USB flash drive that had been on his person at the time of arrest. In front of a room full of investigators, the man grabbed the piece of evidence and stuffed it into his mouth, say witnesses. When he then failed to "pass" the drive for four days, doctors recommended it be surgically removed. The man was charged with obstruction of justice.

Bodies found floating in San Francisco Bay often have shrimp and other creatures in their orifices.

On Christmas Day, 2009, an Ohio man sliced open a potato to discover the shape of a cross inside. And on New Year's Eve of the same year, an Iowa couple found a similar cross inside their own sacred spud. Both couples decided not to eat the holy cross potatoes and posted them for sale on eBay instead.

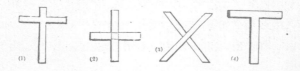

(1)   (2)   (3)   (4)

LUCK OF THE DRAW

In Cave Creek, Arizona, in June 2009, officials decided who got a seat on the town's city council in very unusual fashion. After counting and then recounting, both candidates for the seat received exactly the same number of votes: 660. The Arizona State Constitution allows for a "game of chance" to break the tie, so the two candidates agreed on pulling a card, and the one who drew the higher card would win. Thomas McGuire, in front of a crowd of onlookers, pulled first: the Six of Hearts. Adam Trenk drew second and won the elected seat with the King of Hearts. Locals say that the rolling of dice or drawing of cards has been used to make such decisions a handful of times in the city's past.

In the United States there is more space where nobody is than where anybody is. That is what makes America what it is. —GERTRUDE STEIN, *THE GEOGRAPHICAL HISTORY OF AMERICA*

BEYOND BIZARRE

ORANGE YOU GLAD I DIDN'T SAY BANANA?

In a traditional Hawaiian burial, the body is wrapped in banana, taro, and mulberry leaves before being buried. The traditional funeral meal includes roast pig on banana leaves.

The storme will arise.
And trouble the skies;
This night, and more for the wonder,
The ghost from the Tomb
Affrighted shall come,
Cal'd out by the clap of the Thunder.
—ROBERT HERRICK, "THE HAG"

DOLL PARTS

According to Leslie Rule's *Coast to Coast Ghosts*, a ghoulish collection of haunted tales from across the United States, the paranormal activity at Key West's Artist House Bed and Breakfast centers not around a specter, but on a doll. Robert, the doll, has reportedly moved on his own from room to room, and has also been heard giggling and leering out of windows. If you'd like to meet Robert, he no longer lives at the Artist House, but is now on display at the East Martello Museum, also located in Key West. But the Artist House still experiences strange phenomena, including objects leaping off of shelves and the television turning itself off.

MEDICAL MUSEUM

For the morbidly curious and medically inclined, Dr. Dudley Peter Allen's Dittrick Medical History Museum was created to "preserve the medical heritage of northeastern Ohio by preserving the equipment of its physicians." Located in Cleveland, Ohio, this museum is not for the faint of heart; it includes exhibits such as "The Evils of Nazi Medicine," photograph collections including graphic depictions of various diseases, and case studies in dissection across the centuries, as well as rare books and antique medical instruments.

Every American carries in his bloodstream the heritage of the malcontent and the dreamer. —DOROTHY FULDHEIM, *A THOUSAND FRIENDS*

HANNIBAL'S HIDDEN HORRORS

Dr. Joseph McDowell was a prominent Missouri doctor widely considered to be a brilliant surgeon in 1840s St. Louis. Having taken up residence in Hannibal, Missouri, the doctor also gained a reputation for being eccentric. When his own daughter died as a young girl, he preserved her in a cask and hid the cask in a cave.

He was also a reputed bodysnatcher, who would remove bodies from cemeteries for the purpose of teaching his students medical science—a practice not unusual for doctors of the time. But when the body of a young girl went missing, the townspeople demanded that he return it. McDowell, forewarned by the ghost of his own mother, hid the body before anyone could find it. In addition to his gruesome practices, McDowell was also reputed to keep a pet bear.

The National Museum of Funeral History is located in Houston, Texas, and includes historical information about the culture of funerals in the United States, as well as displays about funerals of such notables as Martin Luther King, Jr., Abraham Lincoln, and Elvis Presley.

Herber Springs, Arkansas, is home to a mortuary museum that features a horse-drawn hearse from 1896, as well as other antique coffins and funerary accoutrements.

THE HAPPIEST OF WIDOWS

The Merry Widows of Nevada City, California, can be seen at most parades and celebrations in this historic mining town located in the foothills of California. They're easily spotted by their Victorian mourning costumes. This charitable group of women in black is most lively at the annual Joe Cain Day parade. Sister widows to the Merry Widows of Joe Cain—a women's mystic society in Mobile, Alabama—they dance through the parade and descend upon Cain's grave to lay flowers upon it. Joe Cain is credited with the birth, or rebirth, of the Mardi Gras celebration.

TAKE THAT

In November 2008, a North Carolina pallbearer was stunned by local sheriffs with Taser guns—during the funeral of his own father. As the coffin was being loaded into the hearse, undercover agents approached the man, who was charged with threatening his ex-wife in another state. When the man resisted arrest (presumably to prevent missing the burial), the officers used their Taser gun on him. Sherriff's officials apologized, agreeing that they should have waited until the end of the funeral to make their arrest.

Americans specially love superlatives. The phrases "biggest in the world," "finest in the world," are on all lips.
—ISABELLA L. BIRD, *A LADY'S LIFE IN THE ROCKY MOUNTAINS*

QUITE A RACK

A New York City woman's meal at a Scandinavian-themed restaurant was rudely interrupted when a 150-pound (68-kg) stuffed moose head, complete with 3-foot-wide (1-meter-wide) antlers, fell on her head.

In December 2009, she filed charges against the restaurant for negligence. At the time of this writing, no settlement had been reached.

In colonial Pennsylvania, it was custom upon the death of the lady of the house to shake up a bottle of vinegar and to turn any barrels, crocks, and jars of stored foods upside down to prevent the deceased from spoiling them.

In the fantastically macabre cookbook *Death Warmed Over: Funeral Food, Rituals, and Customs from Around the World*, author Lisa Rogak recounts several Polish superstitions and beliefs. Among them is the belief that if there is water in the grave, the deceased will be a chronic drunk in the afterlife, and that if you comb you hair with a dead person's comb, your hair will fall out.

TOO MANY DAYS AT SEA

Perhaps they had only one thing on their mind when Spanish explorers named the great state of California after a mythical island called California, which was inhabited only by Amazon women who were ruled by their queen, Califa. The mythical island was described in detail by Garcia Ordonez de Montalvo in his 1510 book *Las Sergas de Esplandián (The Adventures of Esplandián).* Of course, California turned out not to be an island. And perhaps if it had been ruled by women, history may have changed.

SATAN'S CALLING CARD

As of 2008, the state of West Virginia allows members of a small religious group to have their driver's licenses archived on computer databases without the license photos. Citing concerns that bar codes and digitally stored photos are a way of numbering people and thus can lead to "the mark of the beast" (three consecutive sixes), the group petitioned the state. The members of this group do have their photos on their licenses, but the photos themselves are now removed before images of the licenses are stored on computer. One of the members of this same group was fired in 1999 from his job as a schoolteacher when he refused to require his students to wear bar-code identification cards.

In 1900, the president of the United States was paid a salary of $50,000 a year.

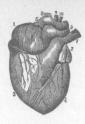

HEARTS AWASH

At a car wash in Paw Paw, Michigan, on a Monday in December 2008, the owner made a startling discovery—an animal heart. The heart was taken to a local veterinarian, who could not determine what creature this solitary organ had come from. It was then brought to a cardiologist, who was unable to rule out the possibility that it was a human heart. Naturally, if it were human, an investigation would be launched. However, the owner of the car wash said if it were, in fact, an animal heart, it would not be the first time animal parts were left behind in his establishment.

HOUSES OF HOAXES

According to its website, "The Museum of Hoaxes is dedicated to promoting knowledge about hoaxes." Located in San Diego, California, the museum also operates a website with extensive archives about historical deceptions, an active blog with up-to-date information, and forums where visitors can discuss hoaxes past and present.

THE GALLERY OF MONSTER TOYS

Raymond Castile created the Gallery of Monster Toys, an online museum "dedicated to preserving a disappearing facet of our popular culture." The gallery's virtual "wings" are divided by era, from the 1960s to the 1990s, and feature items ranging from classic horror-movie souvenirs (such as a mini-guillotine from the 1966 film *Chamber of Horrors)* to whistling, ooky-spooky trees and other unique vintage monster toys. This website, found at *thegalleryofmonstertoys.com,* is sure to delight movie buffs, toy collectors, and fans of the strange alike.

YES, WE HAVE NO BANANAS

The Washington Banana Museum *(bananamuseum.com)* is an online museum dedicated to the beloved yellow fruit. The creator of the website owns and operates Banana Antiques in Auburn, Washington, and the store houses an impressive collection of banana memorabilia.

THE COLORFUL GHOSTS OF CALICO, CALIFORNIA

Located just north of Barstow, California, the town of Calico was once a thriving town of the Wild West.

The riches from a nearby silver mine built the town's streets, hotels, saloons, homes, and requisite houses of ill repute, although Calico had a reputation for being a family-friendly town. Today, this once-thriving town is virtually deserted, but its reputation lives on in the legendary ghosts that make their home there. Miners, schoolchildren, and even town drunks are seen in specter form.

This town is also known for a phenomenon called "the Lights of Calico"—orbs of light that are seen bouncing or moving around the area. You can visit this town, which is just off Interstate 5, ten miles north of Barstow. Logically, you take the Ghost Town Road exit to reach it. Although Bill Cook has retired from leading the historic Calico Ghost Walk, he has left up his website, where you can order his book about the Calico Ghost Walk and the town's ghosts and read about visitors' encounters with the paranormal.

DID YOU KNOW?

A supervolcano lies underneath Yellowstone National Park. According to National Geographic's *The Knowledge Book,* a 37-mile-long, 25-mile-wide, and 6-mile-deep magma chamber containing about 5,800 square miles of magma, boils approximately 5 miles under the earth's surface. An eruption could lead to global climatic catastrophe.

FLAT EARTHERS OR FLATLINERS?

The Flat Earth Society is a group of 21st-century eccentrics who actually believe that the world is flat, despite all scientific and photographic evidence to the contrary. Flat Earthers believe that world space organizations, with their "official" photographs of a spherical earth, are carrying on an elaborate hoax to great profit, says a representative of the organization. Opinions about the actual shape of the earth vary: some Flat Earthers believe it is disk shaped, and others contend that it's infinitely horizontal. Whatever our planet's real shape and size, it's safe to say that the Flat Earth Society is a little out of this world.

FEMUR MADNESS!

A house-hunting couple was in for a fright when they, along with the real estate agent showing them the

Gibson, Louisiana, house, came across a basement full of more than 100 human bones! When the coroner examined the bones, he found that dirt had saturated the marrow inside them—a sign that they were very old, perhaps remains from a Native American burial ground. But how did the bones get piled in the basement? A neighbor claimed that the previous owners of the house would occasionally find a bone while mowing the lawn and began collecting them in the basement. Asset or downside for potential buyers?

STICKY WAVE

You know the phrase "slow as molasses"? Well, molasses not always that slow—and imagine trying to walk through the sticky substance. In 1919, some residents of Boston had to do just that when a vat of the stuff exploded at a distillery. The 50-foot-tall container, which buckled under the pressure of its contents, simply burst, sending a 15-foot-tall wave of molasses shuttling at 35 mph towards unwitting victims, including many of the distillery workers, who were having lunch. They were among the biggest group of fatalities resulting the accident, which ultimately killed 21 people.

SPICY CRIME

A 22-year-old man was arrested in Fresno, California for breaking and entering the home of two farmworkers, rubbing one's face with spices and whacking the other in the head with an eight-inch sausage, then ransacking the workers' house and running away. The money stolen by the thief was recovered, and the alleged assailant presumably given a good grilling by police.

NOTORIOUS CRIMINALS OF NEBRASKA

A 35-year-old man, dubbed the Butt Bandit, was arrested in Valentine, Nebraska, for making imprints of his, ahem, posterior on store windows with petroleum jelly. He was convicted of eight counts of public indecency and one count of disturbing the peace after terrorizing the town for more than two years. He was sentenced to a whopping thirteen and a half months in jail. A word to the wise: make buttprints on your *own* windows instead of going to town.

THERE'S A SILVER LINING TO EVERY CLOUD— EVEN A BOLL WEEVIL CLOUD

Alabama is home to the Boll Weevil Monument, erected in 1919 as a tribute to the cotton-eating pest. Happy-go-lucky farmers in Enterprise, Alabama, took the arrival of the boll weevil as an opportunity to diversify their crops, introducing peanuts and modern agricultural practices to their stagnating farming economy.

 ## PETER PAINLESS

Edgar "Painless" Parker was a trained dentist who brought his practice on the road when business slowed in his native Canada. With the help of one of P. T. Barnum's ex-managers, Parker attracted crowds with his horse-drawn-carriage office, promotional showgirls, and even buglers. The crux of the business was Parker's guarantee that he would painlessly extract a customer's tooth (with the help of a slug of whiskey or an aqueous cocaine he called "hydrocaine") or give them five dollars. He worked with a bucket of pulled teeth at his side, to illustrate how much experience he had. In 1915, Parker was ordered to stop using "Painless" in his name, as it was potentially false advertising. Ever a smart businessman, Parker legally changed his last name to "Painless."

WE CALL 'EM LIP SWEATERS

The American Mustache Institute is a not-for-profit organization that, according to its website, is dedicated to "protecting the rights of, and discrimination against, mustached Americans by promoting the growth, care, and culture of the mustache." Based in St. Louis, the Mustache Institute sponsors events, like the annual 'Stache Bash, honors mustache-wearers with the Robert Goulet Memorial Mustached American of the Year award, and is housed under what it calls the world's largest mustache, the Gateway Arch.

KID HEAVEN

For 14 years, minister Howard Burgess has been building on his 97-foot tree house, the biggest one in the country and maybe the world, on Beehive Lane in Crossville, Tennessee. Supported by an 80-foot oak tree and several smaller trees, the tree house has 80 rooms, including a church and bell tower, and cost only $12,000 to construct. Burgess says that he was inspired to build the tree house one day while he was praying and heard the voice of God tell him, "If you build a tree house, I'll see that you never run out of material." So far, he hasn't.

THE JIMSON WEED OF JAMESTOWN

In Amy Stewart's delightfully deviant *Wicked Plants*, she tells the history of the jimson weed (*Datura stamonium*) and how it helped the American colonists to overthrow British rule. When settlers first arrived on Jamestown Island in 1607, they were drawn to a beautiful but deadly plant. Not knowing that it was poisonous, the new arrivals added the plant to their diet—to horrifying consequences. Among *Datura's* side effects are hallucinations, convulsions, and respiratory failure. But some 70 years later, the survivors of this early ordeal turned their own fate by poisoning the invading British soldiers. The soldiers did not die, but they went insane for several days, allowing the colonists to gain the upper hand. The plant's role gave it the nickname Jamestown weed, which later morphed into jimson weed, its more common name today.

WHY YOU SHOULDN'T INVENT THINGS WHEN YOU'RE DRUNK

On July 2, 1982, an innovator named Larry Walters made the maiden flight of *Inspiration 1*, his homemade aircraft consisting of a lawn chair attached to 45 8-foot, helium-filled weather balloons. Walters brought cargo—a pellet gun, cold beer, and sandwiches. He and his craft eventually reached altitudes of 15,000 feet before Walters shot two balloons and slowly descended, eventually getting entangled in some power lines.

YOUR OWN LITTLE SLICE OF HELL

Residents of Hell, Michigan (all 72 of them), promoted a day very close to their hearts—June 6, 2006 (6/6/06)—by selling "666" memorabilia and one-inch plots of Hell land for the rock-bottom price of $6.66.

Music producer Norwood Young's street-side mansion in Los Angeles is the subject of much neighborhood controversy and even a couple lawsuits. When Young moved in during the mid-90s, he quickly installed 19 replicas of Michelangelo's statue of David—full frontal nudity and all—in the front yard.

BUT HOW IS IT PRONOUNCED?

Nevaeh became the 70th most popular girl's name in 2005 after MTV aired a 2000 interview with Sonny Sandoval, singer of the Christian metal band P.O.D., who named his daughter Nevaeh because it's *heaven* spelled backward.

If you ever see a bunch of people climbing into a manhole in the middle of busy Atlantic Avenue in Brooklyn, don't be alarmed. They're simply tourists visiting one of the borough's lesser-known attractions—the Atlantic Avenue Tunnel, which is all that remains of a failed subway project masterminded by Cornelius Vanderbilt in 1844. The project ended abruptly and under mysterious circumstances when, according to an 1844 newspaper article, the mostly Irish construction workers shot a British contractor who told them they had to work on Sundays. According to the article, the workers hastily buried the contractor's body in the wall of the tunnel, where it presumably still lies today.

The Great Salt Palace in Grand Saline, Texas, is a small house made entirely out of rock salt in tribute to the estimated 16,000-foot-deep salt deposit it sits on top of. The Salt Palace houses a small museum of salt-related oddities, and visitors are given salt crystals free of charge.

If you're ever passing through Tombstone, Arizona, stop for a quick drink at the Bird Cage Theater, which lived a short life as a saloon, theater, and brothel from 1881 to 1889. Wyatt Earp and Doc Holiday played cards there, and it was the site of several murders. (Look closely for bullet holes in the theater and saloon walls.) A destination for ghost-hunters, it's also known as the home of 26 ghosts of former bartenders and customers. Fully restored to its former grandeur, the Bird Cage welcomes visitors for daily tours.

John Gerholt was just another devoted husband until he accidentally—or so he claims—shot his wife, twice, with a sawed-off shotgun. Gerholt was arrested and awaiting trial, and his wife was buried. But Gerholt decided that the woman he couldn't stand in life had, in death, turned into his beloved, and he became obsessed with being buried next to her. From jail, Gerholt managed to forge papers granting him ownership of the burial plot next to the wife that he murdered, so that one day they could rest in peace, together, a happy couple at last.

FROM YOUR LOCAL PAPERS

Here, courtesy of the *Slightly Warped Website (slightlywarped.com)*, are a sampling of real headlines and clippings taken from America's (sorely in need of proofreading) newspapers:

- Department store advertisement: "Get 50% off. Or half price, whichever is less."

- "Statistics Show That Teen Pregnancy Drops Off Significantly After Age 25."

- "One-Armed Man Applauds the Kindness of Strangers."

- From a police log: "A deputy responded to a report of a vehicle stopping at mail boxes. It was the mailman."

- "Fish Need Water, Feds Say."

- "Alton Attorney Accidentally Sues Himself."

- Correction: "Due to incorrect information received from the Clerk of Court's Office, Diane K. Merchant, 38, was incorrectly listed as being fined for prostitution in Wednesday's paper. The charge should have been failure to stop at a railroad crossing. The Public Opinion apologizes for the error."

- From another police log: "At 12:22 PM, a cellular caller reported a large snapping turtle in the roadway at Elm Street and Crescent Road. The turtle fled the area undetected."

- From another police log: "The Learning Center on Hanson Street reports a man across the way stands at his window for hours watching the center, making parents nervous. Police ID the subject as a cardboard cutout of Arnold Schwarzenegger."

- A classified ad: "For Sale: Tombstone. Standard gray. A good buy for someone named Grady."

I THINK YOU HAVE A WRONG NUMBER

The most famous telephone in America resided in the Pacific Bell–owned Mojave phone booth, which was located in the middle of the Mojave Desert. The completely isolated booth, positioned more than 15 miles from interstate highways and miles away from any buildings, attracted a cult following in the 1990s. Soon it was receiving daily phone calls and hundreds of visitors, and had a website dedicated to it. In 2000, the phone company and the National Park Service agreed that the booth should be removed due to environmental degradation caused by constant visitors to the site.

IS THERE A BEN DOVER THERE?

In the long-running TV show *The Simpsons*, bar owner Moe Szyslak is the victim of an ongoing prank orchestrated by young Bart Simpson. Bart phones the bar and asks for a gag name. When Moe calls the name out to the bar, he is enraged to realize that the name is offensive or dirty. It turns out that this running gag is based on a true story that happened in Jersey City in the 1970s.

Two youths, John Elmo and Jim Davidson, repeatedly made similar prank calls to the Tube Bar, owned by former heavyweight boxer Louis "Red" Deutsch. Some of the names they used: Frank N. Stein, Hugh Jass, and Al Killeu.

<hr>

Buzz Aldrin, the second man to walk on the moon after Apollo 11 mission commander Neil Armstrong, gave himself communion in the short time he spent on the surface of the moon, but kept his act secret to avoid controversy. (Formerly, atheist activist Madalyn Murray O'Hair had brought a lawsuit over the reading of Genesis on Apollo 8.) Then a devoted Presbyterian, Aldrin no longer attends religious services, choosing to spend his Sunday mornings at recovery meetings. (Aldrin is a recovering alcoholic and victim of depression.) Aldrin's mother, who committed suicide the year before he walked on the moon, had the maiden name of Moon, but Aldrin kept this fact secret from NASA, not wanting his bosses to think he was trying to gain favor in any way.

✦ THIRTEEN-QUESTION QUIZ ✦

1. What animal can last longer without water than a camel?

2. What animal's dander is believed to be so hallucinogenic that it has been outlawed in nearly a dozen U.S. states?

3. What plant takes its Latin name from Achilles, the mighty Greek warrior whose only weakness was the back of his heel?

4. Who was the first human cannonball?

5. What famous inventor had a fascination with the paranormal?

6. What are the seven wonders of the ancient world?

7. What famous queen had a morbid love for her husband?

8. What convicted serial killer once held a job in a chocolate factory?

9. What famous rocker once held a job as a gravedigger?

10. What former U.S. president's corpse was moved 18 times?

11. What is basophobia?

12. What did the Bateson Revival Device prevent?

13. What ailment did Attila the Hun die from?

Answers appear on page 302.

SOURCES

BOOKS

Acton, Johnny, Tania Adams, and Matt Packer. *Origin of Everyday Things*. New York: Sterling Publishing, 2006.

Adler, Freda, and G. O. W. Mueller. *Outlaws of the Ocean*. New York: Hearst Marine Books, 1985.

Ash, Russell. *Firefly's World of Facts*. Richmond Hill, Ontario: Firefly Books, 2007.

Bakalar, Nicholas. *The Medicine Cabinet of Curiosities*. New York: Henry Holt. 2009.

Belanger, Jeff. *Encyclopedia of Haunted Places*. Franklin Lakes, NJ: New Page Books, 2005.

Benoit, Todd. *Where Are They Buried? How Did They Die?* New York: Black Dog & Leventhal, 2003.

Biggs, Mary. *The Columbia Book of Quotations by Women*. New York: Columbia University Press, 1996.

Boese, Alex. *The Museum of Hoaxes*. New York: Dutton, 2002.

Bondeson, Jan. *The Two-Headed Boy and Other Medical Maladies*. Ithaca, NY: Cornell University Press, 2000.

Bradley, Mickey, and Dan Gordon. *Haunted Baseball*. Guilford, CT: The Lyons Press, 2007.

Braithwaite, Daniel. *Fairground Architecture: The World of Amusement Parks, Carnivals, and Fairs*. New York: Frederick A. Prager, 1968.

Bravo, Leonore M. *Rabbit Skin Blanket: About the Washo of the Eastern Sierra and Their Neighbors, The Paiute*. Hanover, PA: Braun-Brumfield Inc., 1991.

Brewer's Dictionary of Phrase and Fable. New York: Harper and Row, 1989.

Bright, Michael. *There Are Giants in the Sea: Monsters and Mysteries of the Depths Explored*. London: Robson Books, 1989.

Buckland, Raymond. *The Weiser Field Guide to Ghosts*. San Francisco: Weiser Books, 2009.

Budd, Deena West. *The Weiser Field Guide to Cryptozoology*. San Francisco: Weiser Books, 2010.

Cavendish, Richard, ed. *Encyclopedia of the Unexplained: Magic, Occultism, and Parapsychology*. New York: McGraw-Hill, 1974.

Cavendish, Richard. *The World of Ghosts and the Supernatural*. New York: Facts on File, 1994.

Colman, Penny. *Corpses, Coffins, and Crypts: A History of Burial*. New York: Henry Holt, 1997.

Conley, Craig. *Magic Words: A Dictionary*. San Francisco: Weiser Books, 2008.

Dolson, Sylvia. *Bear-Ology: Fascinating Bear Facts, Tales, and Trivia*. Masonville, CO: PixyJack Press, 2009.

Engright, D.J. *The Oxford Book of the Supernatural*. New York: Oxford University Press, 1995

Felleman, Hazel. *The Best Loved Poems of the American People*. New York: Doubleday, 1936

Guetebier, Amber and Brenda Knight. *The Poetry Oracle*. San Francisco: CCC Publishing, 2008.

Haggard, Howard W. *Devils, Drugs, and Doctors: The Story of the Science of Healing from Medicine-Man to Doctor*. New York: Harper and Row, 1929.

Holzer, Hans. *Travel Guide to Haunted Houses*. New York: Black Dog & Leventhal. 1998.

Horn, Stacy. *Unbelievable*. New York: HarperCollins, 2009.

Howe, Randy. *Flags of the Fifty States and Their Incredible Histories*. Guilford, CT: Globe Pequot, 2004.

Howe, W. H. *Everybody's Book of Epitaphs*. Kent, England: Pryor Publications, 1995.

Inter-tribal Council of Nevada. *Numa: A Northern Paiute History*. Salt Lake City, UT: University of Utah Printing Service, 1976.

Jawyer, Michael. The Anatomy of a Haunting. *Spritiuality and Health*. March/April 2010. Volume 13, No 2.

Journal of Anthropological Research, Volume 46. Number 3-Fall.

Karg, Barb, and Arjean Spaite. *The Everything Pirates Book*. Avon, MA: Adams Media, 2007.

Kenner, Corrine, and Craig Miller. *Strange but True*. St. Paul, MN: Llewellyn, 1999.

Knaebel, Nathaniel. *Step Right Up: Stories of Carnivals, Sideshows, and the Circus*. New York: Carroll & Graff, 2004.

Lankford, Andrea. *Haunted Hikes: Spine-Tingling Tales and Trails from North America's National Parks*. Santa Monica, CA: Santa Monica Press, 2006.

Lapica, R. L. *Facts of File Yearbook, Volume II: 1942*. New York: Person's Index, 1943.

Largo, Michael. *Final Exits: The Illustrated Encyclopedia of How We Die*. New York, HarperCollins, 2006.

Macinnis, Peter. *Poisons*. New York: Arcade Publishing, 2004.

Marrs, Jim. *Above Top Secret*. New York: Disinformation, 2008.

Masoff, Joy. *Oh, Yuck! The Encyclopedia of Everything Nasty*. New York: Workman Publishing, 2000.

McLain, Bill. *Do Fish Drink Water? Puzzling and Improbable Questions and Answers*. New York: William Morrow & Company, 1999.

Moodie, Roy L. *The Antiquity of Disease*. Chicago: University of Chicago Press, 1923.

Murrell, Deborah. *Superstitions: 1013 of the Wackiest Myths, Fables, and Old Wives' Tales*. Pleasantville, NY: Reader's Digest, 2008.

National Geographic Society. *The Knowledge Book: Everything You Need to Know to Get by in the 21st Century*. Washington, D.C.: National Geographic Society, 2007.

New Scientist. *Does Anything Eat Wasps?* New York: Free Press, 2005.

Newman, Stanley, and Hal Fittipaldi. *15,003 Answers*. New York: Random House, 2007.

Nickell, Joe. *Secrets of the Sideshows*. Lexington: University Press of Kentucky, 2005.

Panati, Charles. *Panati's Extraordinary Origins of Everyday Things*. New York: Harper & Row, 1987.

Pearson, Will, Mangesh Hattikudur, and Elizabeth Hunt. *mental_floss Presents: Forbidden Knowledge: A Wickedly Smart Guide to History's Naughtiest Bits*. New York: HarperCollins, 2005.

Porter, Roy. *Blood & Guts: A Short History of Medicine*. New York: Norton and Company, 2002.

Ramsland, Katherine. *Cemetery Stories: Haunted Graveyards, Embalming Secrets, and the Life of a Corpse After Death*. New York: HarperCollins, 2001.

Randi, James. *An Encyclopedia of Claims, Frauds, and Hoaxes of the Occult and Supernatural*. New York: St. Martin's, 1997.

Ray, C. Claiborne. *The New York Times Second Book of Science Questions and Answers*. New York: Anchor Books, 2002.

Reader's Digest. *Stories Behind Everyday Things*. Pleasantville, NY: Reader's Digest Association, 1980.

Reader's Digest. *The Reader's Digest Great Encyclopedic Dictionary*. Pleasantville, NY: Reader's Digest Association, 1966.

Reader's Digest. *Unseen World: The Science, Theories, and Phenomena Behind Paranormal Events*. Pleasantville, NY: Reader's Digest Association, 2008.

Roach, Mary. *Six Feet Over: Adventures in the Afterlife*. Edinburgh, Scotland: Canongate, 2007.

Robertson, Sandy. *The Illustrated Beast: The Aleister Crowley Scrapbook*. Boston: Weiser Books, 2002.

Rogak, Lisa. *Death Warmed Over: Funeral Food, Rituals, and Customs from Around the World*. Berkeley, CA: Ten Speed Press, 2004.

Rule, Leslie. *Coast to Coast Ghosts: True Stories of Hauntings Across America*. Kansas City, MO: Andrews McMeel, 2001.

Ruoff, Henry W. *The Century Book of Facts*. Springfield, MA: King-Richardson Company, 1900.

Sanders, Jack. *The Secrets of Wild Flowers*.Essex, CT: Lyons Press, 2010

Schechter, Harold. *The Whole Death Catalog*. New York: Random House, 2009.

Schott, Ben. *Schott's Almanac: 2007*. New York: Bloomsbury, 2008.

Schutt, Bill. *Dark Banquet: Blood and the Curious Life of Blood-Feeding Creatures*. New York: Harmony Books, 2008.

Schutt, Bill. *Dark Banquet: Blood and the Curious Lives of Blood-Feeding Creatures*. New York: Harmony Books, 2008.

Scientific American. *Scientific American's Ask the Experts*. New York: HarperCollins, 2003.

Scott, Beth, and Michael Norman. *Haunted Heartland*. New York: Barnes & Noble, 1985.

Spence, Lewis. *An Encyclopedia of Occultism*. New York: University Books, 1968.

Stein, Gordon. *The Encyclopedia of the Paranormal*. Amherst, NY: Prometheus Books, 1996.

Stewart, Amy. *Wicked Plants*. Chapel Hill, North Carolina: Algonquin Books, 2009.

Stewart, George R. *Ordeal by Hunger: The Classic Story of The Donner Party*. New York City: Pocket Books, 1971.

Taylor, Troy. *Field Guide to Haunted Graveyards*. Alton, IL: Whitechapel Productions Press, 2003.

Varhola, Michael J. *Shipwrecks and Lost Treasures, Great Lakes*. Guilford, CT: Globe Pequot Press, 2008.

Ventura, Varla. *The Book of the Bizarre*. San Francisco: Weiser Books, 2008.

Villiers, Alan. *Posted Missing*. New York: Charles Scribner's Sons, 1974.

Violini, Juanita Rose. *Almanac of the Infamous, the Incredible, and the Ignored*. San Francisco: Weiser Books, 2009.

Waldron, H. A.. "Did the Mad Hatter Have Mercury Poisoning?" *British Medical Journal (Clinical Research Edition)* 287 (December 24–31, 1982): 6409. Originally published in 1961.

Watts, D. C. *The Dictionary of Plant Lore*. Maryland Heights, MO: Academic Press, 2007

Webster, Richard. *The Encyclopedia of Superstitions*. Woodbury, MN: Llewellyn, 2008.

Wetzel, Charles. *Haunted U.S.A.* New York: Sterling Publishing, 2008.

Wilson, Colin. *Unsolved Mysteries: Past and Present*. Chicago: Contemporary Books, 1992.

Yolen, Jane. *Sea Queens: Women Pirates Around the World*. Watertown, MA: Charlesbridge, 2008.

WEBSITES

americasblood.org
atlasobscura.com
beerfacts.net
bleachereport.com
brilliantdreams.com
calicoghostwalk.com
crime.about.com
dailymail.co.uk
deepseamonsters.com
deuceofclubs.com
dictionary.com
eternalreefs.com
factsmonk.com
farnsworthhouseinn.com
fearseekerfiles.com
funshun.com
generalpatton.org
history.navy.mil
kapucini.cz
killerplants.com
moviemaker.com

movies.lovetoknow.com
museumofhoaxes.com
museumstuff.com
neatorama.com
nyt.com
octopus.com
oqoxfordjournals.com
orkneyjar.com
pbase.com
prairieghosts.com
rd.com
scienceray.com
tarahill.com
thesmokinggun.com
unsolvedmysteries.com
usatoday.com
wapedia.mobi
wikipedia.com
wired.com
ncbi.nlm.nih.gov
zooped.com

ACKNOWLEDGMENTS

Special thanks to my editors Rachel Leach and Amber Guetebier, without whom this book would not exist. Thanks also to the fantastic staff at Weiser Books: Susie Pitzen, Jan Johnson, Donna Linden, Jordan Overby, Bonni Hamilton, and Caroline Pincus. Heartfelt gratitude to Sara Gillingham whose design on this book thrills and chills me! Humble gratitude to the dynamic and brilliant Hilary Smith and for the boundless support of Allyson May. A big thanks to the outstanding interns Jillian Garcia, Geneva Vander Poel, Kristina Anderson, and Martha Knauf. Undying gratitude and thanks to contributors and supporters: Pirate Chris Ward, Alix "Ghost-Eyes" Anderson, Johnny Ola and his beautiful wife Lizzy Lee Savage, "Zooboy" Ken Pelto, the enchanting Mistress of the Sword Lia Carotta, Wendy the Witch and DJ Craz-E and their shimmering offspring: Jacob, Emma, and Ida Hunter, Art Amiss, Nicole Rollergirl Makris, and of course, Phillip and the Zombie.

✥ ANSWERS TO QUIZ ✥

Answers:

1. The rat.

2. The duck.

3. *Achillea millifolium*, or yarrow.

4. Zazel, a 14-year-old girl with the London Circus.

5. Thomas Alva Edison.

6. The pyramids at Giza, the statue of Zeus at Olympia, the hanging gardens of Babylon, the colossus of Rhodes, the lighthouse of Alexandria, the temple of Artemis at Ephesus, and the mausoleum at Halicarnassus.

7. The Spanish queen Juana, whose husband Phillip died in 1506. She kept his coffin with her for the rest of her life.

8. Jeffrey Dahmer.

9. The one and only Rod Stewart.

10. Abraham Lincoln's.

11. Basophobia is the fear of standing up or attempting to walk; it stems mainly from a fear of falling.

12. Premature burial or being buried alive.

13. A nosebleed.

For more terrifying trivia and hilariously horrifying facts, check out Varla Ventura's *The Book of the Bizarre*, available now wherever books are sold.

TO OUR READERS

Weiser Books, an imprint of Red Wheel/Weiser, publishes books across the entire spectrum of occult and esoteric subjects. Our mission is to publish quality books that will make a difference in people's lives without advocating any one particular path or field of study. We value the integrity, originality, and depth of knowledge of our authors.

Our readers are our most important resource, and we appreciate your input, suggestions, and ideas about what you would like to see published. Please feel free to contact us to request our latest book catalog, or to be added to our mailing list.

Red Wheel/Weiser, LLC
500 Third Street, Suite 230
San Francisco, CA 94107
www.redwheelweiser.com